IN THE PICOS
DE EUROPA

IN THE PICOS
DE EUROPA

On foot, on horseback, by bicycle, by car and by 4WD

Vicente Ena Álvarez

Amelia Álvarez Cerezales

Edilesa

Editor in chief: Vicente Pastor

Lay-out: Vicente Pastor and Joaquín Alegre

Proofs of the Spanish edition read by: Elena Hidalgo

Photocomposition and Infographics: Letter MAC

Photomechanics: Base 5

Printed by: C.G. Otzarreta

English Translation: Gordon Keitch

Photographs: Manuel Martín (6, 8-9, 20a, 21a, 28a, 33, 35, 36, 37, 38, 41, 42, 45, 46, 48, 51, 53, 55, 56b, 57, 58, 62-63, 65, 66, 69, 70, 78-79, 82, 83, 84, 86, 87, 88, 89, 90, 91, 92, 93, 96, 97, 98, 100-101, 102, 105, 106, 118, 130a, 132, 133, 134-135, 136-137, 140b, 144, 146, 147, 148, 150-151, 152-153, 155, 156b, 158-159, 170a, 172, 176b, 176c, 178b, 181, 182, 183, 184-185, 188, 189b, 194, 196, 197, 198, 210, 212-213, 214a, 221). Vicente Ena (21b, 23, 28b, 29, 50, 52, 56a, 72-73, 75, 131b, 140a, 140c, 142, 143, 148-149, 162, 165, 169, 170b, 174, 175, 176a, 178a, 186, 189a, 195). Miguel Sánchez y Puri Lozano (Portada, 2, 13, 24-25, 26, 47, 61, 110, 113, 114, 116, 119, 120-121, 122, 124, 138, 156a, 162, 166, 168, 192, 207, 208, 214b, 220). Valentín Costo (13, 14-15, 16-17, 50, 52, 109, 200, 202-203, 204, 209, 216-217, 218-219, 223, 224). Norberto (20b, 32, 131a). Vicente Pastor (54, 130b).

© *Texte:* Vicente Ena Alvarez

© EDILESA
General Sanjurjo, 7 - 24001 León (Spain)
Telephone: 987 22 10 66 or (intl) + 34-87-22 10 66

1st Edition, 1995

Paperback: I.S.B.N.: 84-8012-117-3
Depósito Legal: LE-787-1996
Printed in Spain. Impreso en España

CONTENTS

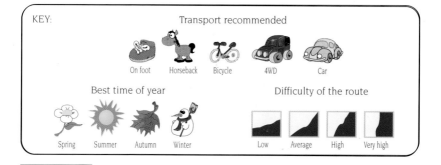

Facing page: The Cares Gorge. • *Following double page:* Ándara from Santo Toribio.

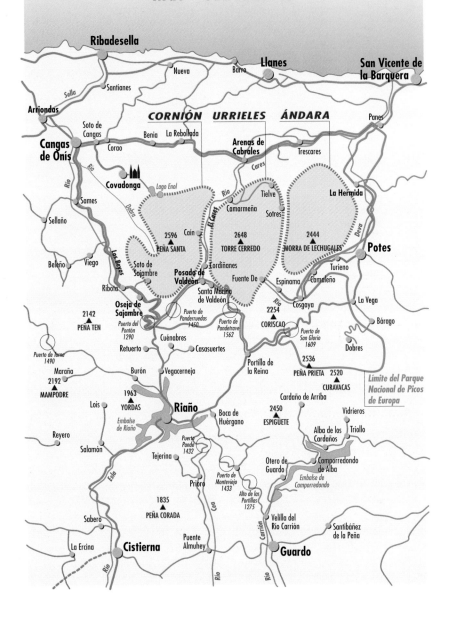

Mar Cantábrico

Ribadesella

Nueva Barro Llanes

San Vicente de la Barquera

Santianes

Sella

Arriondas

Soto de Cangas

Cangas de Onís

Corao

Benia La Rebollada

CORNIÓN URRIELES ÁNDARA

Panes

Arenas de Cabrales

Trescares

Río

Cares

Covadonga *Lago Enol*

Tielve

La Hermida

Sames

Dobra

Río

El Cares

Camarmeña

Sotres

Sellaño

2596 Caín
▲
PEÑA SANTA

2648
▲
TORRE CERREDO

2444
▲
MORRA DE LECHUGALES

Deva

Potes

Beleño Viego

Soto de Sajambre

Los Beyos

Cordiñanes

Posada de Valdeón

Fuente De

Espinama

Camaleño

Turieno

La Vega

Ribota

Santa Marina de Valdeón

Río

Cosgaya

Oseja de Sajambre

2142
▲
PEÑA TEN

Puerto del Pontón 1290

Puerto de Panderruedas 1450

Puerto de Pandetrave 1562

2254
▲
CORISCAO

Bárago

Cuénabres

Puerto de San Glorio 1609

Retuerto Casasuertes

Dobres

Puerto de Torno 1490

Maraña
2192
▲
MAMPODRE

Burón Vegacerneja

Portilla de la Reina

2536
PEÑA PRIETA 2520
▲

CURAVACAS

Lois
1963
▲
YORDAS

Riaño

Cardaño de Arriba

Límite del Parque Nacional de Picos de Europa

Embalse de Riaño

Boca de Huérgano

2450
ESPIGÜETE

Vidrieros

Reyero

Puerto Pando 1432

Alba de los Cardaños

Triollo

Salamón

Tejerina

Otero de Guardo

Camporredondo de Alba

Puerto de Monteviejo 1433

Prioro

Embalse de Camporredondo

Alto de las Portillas 1275

1835
▲
PEÑA CORADA

Cea

Velilla del Río Carrión

Carrión

Santibáñez de la Peña

Sabero

Puente Almuhey

La Ercina

Cistierna

Guardo

Río

INTRODUCTION

One

Every guide or book has to have a backbone, one or two ideas that the author wishes to transmit to the readers so that they can actually take part in its production.

This guide book does not only set out to give the reader information about a network of routes through spectacular landscapes, but also to instil in him the spirit of admiration and respect for Nature of those pioneers whose boundless efforts have revealed to us the full marvel of the Picos de Europa.

Among the legendary figures associated with the conquest of the summits, three stand out from the rest, each one with his own unique personal qualities that have led him to stand the test of time.

The Count of Saint-Saud was a French aristocrat who spent many hours of his life in these parts, slight of body and restless of mind, and overflowing with a vitality that allowed him to climb crags at sixty-five and to ride along tracks on horseback at ninety-five. To him we owe the accurate measurements of the peaks and a superb topographical map of the region. In his delightful book *Por los Picos de Europa*, technical matters aside, he comes over as an eloquent recorder of life, able to capture exactly the Spanish national character of the day, calling this region the land of patience, because of the delays to which guides and porters were forever subject.

Pedro Pidal, the Marquis of Villaviciosa, the author of count-less studies of these mountains, a good climber and uncondi-tional admirer of the beauty of the Picos de Europa, was the first to set foot on the summit of Mt Naranjo of Bulnes and enjoyed telling the tale of his feat in his book *Picos de Europa*.

Gregorio Pérez Demaria, the *Cainejo*, an inhabitant of Caín and a chamois hunter, though short in stature, had enormous physical strength. He went up with Pedro Pidal in the historic conquest of the summit, climbing barefoot all the way as he felt he gripped the rock more securely like that.

These lines are obviously not enough to recognize the merits of these and other people so closely related with Picos, but their way of life and of interpreting their surroundings should be emulated by any visitors who today, tomorrow or any day may become Picos adventurers, in the knowledge that on any day one may become a real discoverer. The Picos de Europa, which according to legend owe their name to the moment when an Asturian prince married his beloved Europa on Mount Vindius after abducting her from her father, the Phoenician king Agenor, form a mountain range set in the central area of the Cantabrian Chain.

These limestone massifs vary greatly in height, from 90 metres at the River Cares to the 2,648 metres of Torre Cerredo. It is a geographically varied area if ever there was one, for everything imaginable is brought together there in an unpredic-table sequence of immense slopes, forests, valleys, depressions, caves, streams and peaks as sharp-pointed as swords, the whole condimented with a varied flora and rich fauna visible at every step. Another important aspect of the region is its culture and folk tradition, which shape rural architectural forms with a traditional flavour, as are our dealings with the people, accents intermingling without ever forgetting their origin, and where the affable character of the locals and shepherds fills hours with conversation when we break for a rest, while they are also a reliable source of information, as they know the most out-of-the-way trails.

From the geographical point of view, the Picos de Europa are

Facing page: The ascent to the Horcados Rojos Col.
Following double page: Mt Llambrión and La Palanca from Torre Cerredo.

made up of three huge massifs separated by fast-flowing rivers of clear water.

The *Western Massif* comprises the so-called Covadonga Mountains or Cornión Peaks, bordered by the rivers Sella and Cares. It is home to the Covadonga National Park, with its famous lakes, Enol and La Ercina. Here also are the Peña Santa de Castilla ("Holy Crag of Castile", 2,596 m.), Torre de Santa María ("St Mary's Tower", 2,486 m.), Torre Bermeja ("Red Tower", 2,400 m.) and Torre Parda ("Brown Tower", 2,314 m.), the most important heights, while there are also a great many lower peaks, which are no less spectacular, such as the Pico las Vidriosas (1,360 m.), the Torres de Cotalbín (2,187 m.), the Pico Conjurtao (1,924 m.) or the Pico Cotalba (2,026 m.). Each has its own characteristics that make it unique and unforgettable, offering the traveller the opportunity to enjoy the adventure according to his budgets of time and physical fitness.

The *Central Massif*, or *Urrieles Massif*, is bordered by the Cares and Duje rivers. Here stands the mythical Mt Naranjo of Bulnes (2,519 m.), a perpetual challenge to the most daring climbers and an unforgettable sight for any visitor who should contemplate its vertical arêtes, its smooth and interminable faces, its challenge to the sky itself. Other famous names are the Torre del Oso ("Bear Tower", 2,460 m.), Las Moñetas (2,554 m.) or Mt Tiro Navarro (2,604 m.).

It is here that we find the highest summits in Picos, many of them over 2,600 m., such as Torre Cerredo (2,648 m), Torre de Llambrión (2,642 m.), Tiro Tirso (2,641 m.) and Peña Vieja ("Old Crag", 2,613 m.), making the appearance of this Massif more rugged than any, and it frightens us to think how our legs might respond should we ever wish to crown one of its summits. Espinama and Camarmeña are the villages guarding the northern and southern entrances respectively, and therefore compulsory stopping places.

The *Eastern*, or *Ándara Massif* is bathed by the waters of the Duje and the Deva. Its smaller area and lower peaks in no way lessen the charm of this sector, where Potes is the natural meet-

---

Preceding double page: Summit of Torre Cerredo *(top left).* Treasurer's Peak from Horcados Rojos *(bottom left).* The way to Jermoso Col *(top left).* Climbing the Holy Crag *(bottom right).*

ing place, with its incredible atmosphere in summer. Mt Morra de Lechugales (2,444 m.), the Sagrado Corazón ("Sacred Heart", 2,212 m.), Pico Cortés (2,370 m.), Pica del Jierro (2,426 m.) and Prao Cortés (2,287 m.) are the main names giving rise to as many hikes around an area always untamed and changing, where the weather switches from sun to rain in an instant, or from calm to storm, taking us by surprise with a sky as blue as a luminous canvass or a cloud so thick it denies us visibility down to our own feet. Despite all this, or perhaps because of it, the Picos de Europa will always be an enigma and a constant source of surprises.

The Picos de Europa are made up of the so-called mountain limestones, laid down about three hundred million years ago. Tectonic folding and contraction processes brought about considerable elevations and depressions, giving the area its rugged appearance. Later on, the Quaternary glaciations finished off the remodelling of the area, forming glacial moraines, which would then give way to the excavation of river valleys, while certain peculiar formations appeared, the *llambrías*, or rock faces polished by the ice to make surfaces as smooth as mirrors. Glaciation produced erosion in some areas to create thus the conditions for the later formation over time of hundreds of lakes, which are now the corries, or *jous*, an unmistakable characteristic of the region. The wearing away of the limestone and the action of water have created a fantastic network of caves here, with a great variety of size and depth, giving great opportunities to an incipient speleology, a less known facet of the Picos.

One should have some idea, albeit a very general one, of the climate before making plans to explore the area. The northern slopes, next to the sea, are characterized by higher humidity and rainfall (over 1,400 mm. at La Hermida), while the southern slopes are drier. To this must be added the effect of height, from almost sea level up to over 2,600 metres.

This creates, according to the experts, a set of bioclimatic floors (altitude bands), characterized by temperature and vegeta-

---

Following double page: Some of the best known observation areas in the Picos: Cable *(top left)*, El Oso (Bear Observation Area) *(bottom left)*, El Tombo *(top right)*, King's Observation Area *(bottom right)*.

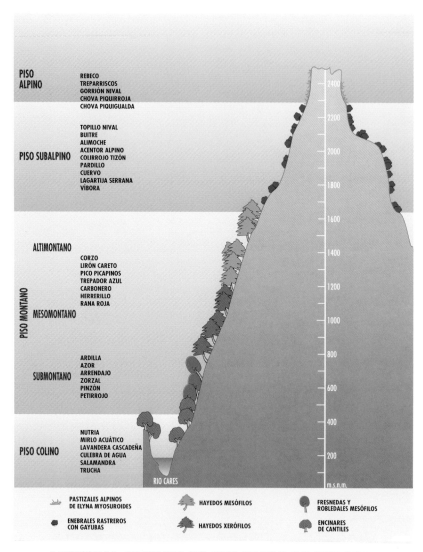

PISO
ALPINO
REBECO
TREPARRISCOS
GORRIÓN NIVAL
CHOVA PIQUIRROJA
CHOVA PIQUIGUALDA

PISO SUBALPINO
TOPILLO NIVAL
BUITRE
ALIMOCHE
ACENTOR ALPINO
COLIRROJO TIZÓN
PARDILLO
CUERVO
LAGARTIJA SERRANA
VÍBORA

PISO MONTANO

ALTIMONTANO

MESOMONTANO
CORZO
LIRÓN CARETO
PICO PICAPINOS
TREPADOR AZUL
CARBONERO
HERRERILLO
RANA ROJA

SUBMONTANO
ARDILLA
AZOR
ARRENDAJO
ZORZAL
PINZÓN
PETIRROJO

PISO COLINO
NUTRIA
MIRLO ACUÁTICO
LAVANDERA CASCADEÑA
CULEBRA DE AGUA
SALAMANDRA
TRUCHA

RIO CARES

m.s.n.m.

PASTIZALES ALPINOS
DE ELYNA MYOSUROIDES

HAYEDOS MESÓFILOS

FRESNEDAS Y
ROBLEDALES MESÓFILOS

ENEBRALES RASTREROS
CON GAYUBAS

HAYEDOS XERÓFILOS

ENCINARES
DE CANTILES

VERTICAL SECTION OF THE PICOS DE EUROPA
SHOWING FLORA AND FAUNA ASSOCIATED WITH DIFFERENT HEIGHTS
[From Rivas *et al* (1984), Ediciones Leonesas]

This page: Section of the Picos showing heights.
Facing page: Asphodel and red satyrion *(top)*, Broom and gentian *(bottom)*.

tion. There are four easily recognized bioclimatic floors in the Picos de Europa. The Alpine one (over 2,200 m.) is characterized by a mean annual temperature under $3^{o}C$, snowfalls are frequent from October to June and conditions in winter are

This page: One of the most beautiful flowers of Cantabria: *Aster alpinus.*
Preceding double page: The bear: myth and relic of Iberia's fauna.

extremely harsh and dangerous, with frequent avalanches. We cannot speak of perpetual snows at this level but we can mention the permanent snowfields on Torre Cerredo and on Mt Llambrión, which remain even in the driest and hottest summers. Lichens and mosses hardly cling to the rocks and only a thin pasture occurs in the most favourable areas. Next is the Sub-Alpine floor, between the 1,700 and 2,200-m. contours, with a mean annual temperature between 3 and 7°C. It is abundant in junipers and gorses, with extensive pastures frequently visited by chamois and livestock (goats and sheep), which often overgraze, contributing to soil erosion. Then comes the montane zone, between 500 and 1,700 m., with mean annual temperatures from 7 to 12°C, where the best known vegetation is to be found, with extensive beech, oak and ash woods. It is woodland *par excellence*, where wildlife is represented by two stars: the brown bear and the Cantabrian capercaillie. Last is the colline floor, below 500 m., with mean annual temperatures over 12°. The vegetation is different from that of the previous zones, with holm oak woods and gallery forests along the rivers, and pastureland won by man from the forest in days gone by.

Fog is common in the Picos, and should be born in mind by hillwalkers, as apart from not letting us enjoy the scenery, it can almost certainly disorientate us and make us lose our way even on the best-known routes. The sea of clouds is an unforgettable sight, when above 1,300-1,600 metres there is brilliant sunshine and below, a thick fog allowing the identification of peaks as islands of pure rock in the moving white sea of clouds.

In each massif mountaineers will find refuges, the step before the final assault on the colossus of the day, and for the less adventurous there are established campsites, other areas where camping is allowed, and a variety of inns and guest-houses in all the towns and villages, as well as a high-quality and very varied gastronomy.

Following double page: The Picos de Europa Regional Park is home to a rich and varied fauna: Chamois *(top left)*, small tortoiseshell butterfly *(bottom left)*, capercaillie *(top right)* and wheatear *(bottom right)*.

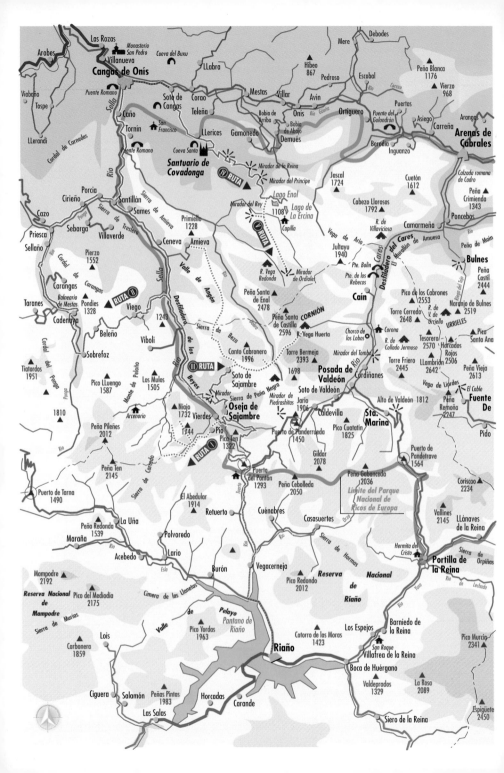

TOWARDS LOS BEYOS

Two

RIAÑO - VEGACERNEJA - PONTÓN PASS - OSEJA DE SAJAMBRE - LOS BEYOS -
SAMES - SANTILLÁN - CANGAS DE ONÍS

56 km

After leaving Riaño, this route is feasible for the dyed-in-the-wool cyclist, as almost all of it is downhill, once we have climbed the Pontón Pass (really quite a gentle climb, anyway).

The new Riaño (see p. 37) has the appearance of a modern tourist centre, combining new buildings with the stone church on the square. Little by little it is becoming populated and is offering services to the traveller, who will find places to stay at, together with a variety of outings to unique spots.

The road winds away towards Vegacerneja, past great slopes where the beechwoods change colour with the seasons. Heath and broom take up the deforested parts of the slopes, with pastures in the lower parts of the valleys. Daffodils, orchids, white asphodels and buttercups are among the flowers that always brighten up the meadows. We often find roe deer at sunrise and sunset, as the peace of this protected area makes them lose some of their shyness and they come out into the traveller's view. This valley is one of the tailbacks of the reservoir and is a meeting place for anglers seeking the peace of the mountains, the green of the pasturelands and the possibility of catching the sought-after trout.

After Vegacerneja, we go up the old road, which is narrower, following the valley gradually up to the wayside chapel of the Pontón, which is surrounded by green meadows which are tinted yellow every spring; it is almost a ritual to watch as the daffodils take over the grasslands and yellow becomes the dominant colour.

On reaching the Pontón Height (1,290 m.), we have to stop to see the crags of the Llavaris Pass, the way into the Sajambre Valley. The bare rock contrasts with the beechwoods covering the valley floor, a splendid foretaste of what awaits us. The undergrowth is made up of bilberry and strawberry, which leave room for the service trees and holly dotted around.

The road winds down through hairpin bends among the beeches, which filter the sun's rays on a clear day or trace out fantastic shapes in the fog. Soon we come to a stream that goes almost unnoticed; it's the Sella, which rises at the Fuente del Infierno ("Hell Spring"), known for the coldness of its waters, a

This page: The New Riaño • *Facing page:* Oseja de Sajambre, traditional and welcoming.

good place to stop for lunch, pick up the wrappers (rule number one for every traveller is never to leave any trace of his passage) and then carry on. From an especially sharp bend, the Petenera, a path leads off to the left which is not negotiable for cars but which allows the walker to go a few hundred metres to see the wide valley the Sella flows down on its way to Pica Ten, the guardian of Oseja de Sajambre and abundant in roe deer, which graze in the surrounding meadows. Beech, hazel, rowan and holly are our fellow-travellers, the occasional jay crossing our path and brightening up the atmosphere with its colour.

The dense wood of beech trees comes to an end to give way to open spaces, where the meadowland stretches from the valley up the slopes, dotted with ancient trees that offer shade in summer, with the limestone ever present in the highest crags. In this ever-changing landscape, the journey can never be boring.

Oseja is a large village, the capital of the valley and a tourist spot. Its mild climate makes it very busy every summer, as it is the starting point for a variety of outings. The church is a very solid construction, big, well looked after and overlooking a valley where some of the houses seem to hang from invisible threads.

After Oseja we cross the River Buseco, which soon flows into the Sella, to reach Ribota, which is a little off the road, but worth a visit, as it is the centre of the area's livestock tradition, carried on amid spacious and fertile meadows covered every spring in daffodils and other flowers.

A DEAD-END GORGE?...LOS BEYOS

11 km

The road gets narrower and more winding, and the mountains seem to block the car's path. We are entering the Los Beyos Canyon, a gorge 11 kilometres long that the river has turned into quite a spectacle. Oak, ash, maple, hazel, plum, lime and elm mingle everywhere, giving variety to a scenery wedged between steep slopes so close together that we could almost jump across. Although the bends are sharp, there are lay-bys where we can leave the car and enjoy the scenery in peace. In one of these places there is an old maple tree with almost horizontal roots, just right for resting a foot on (with the utmost care) and looking down into the spectacularly gouged gorge with the Sella at the bottom, a long way down, but the view is worth the risk. During the spring thaw large quantities of water come cascading down from above hurtling against the stone and bouncing off in a thousand drops that refresh the air and bestow a special kind of joy on this route. A few minutes later we are down almost to the level of the river, but this does not make the scenery any less important, as the limestone keeps trying to strangle the road with its immensity.

It is a place to contemplate in silence but with the eyes wide open for every detail of a tree hanging in space, stones hailing down when washed away by rain or kicked away by the goats that walk along tracks narrower than knife edges, the reflections of the limestone after rain, the butterflies incessantly visi-

---

Facing page: San Pedro Fall, Soto de Sajambre.

ting the blossom or the sounds that the river itself amplifies as its leaps among the rocks.

Then, after the Vidoso bridge, along the gorge, we reach Ceneya and go past the Dobra power station on the way to Sames. During the drive we've changed provinces, from León to Asturias, but not sceneries, as the gorge is long and narrow all the way, although it gets gentler towards the end to give way to wide open green meadows, always dotted with trees, where the presence of cows is unbroken.

Along the gorge there are bars selling Los Beyos cheese, home-made from cow's milk with an aromatic and somewhat dry flavour, but not too strong on the palate, and which could well serve as a fitting end to a fine meal.

The valley continually widens, with pastureland as the backbone of the landscape and the River Sella swollen by its tributaries, to reach Caño, another compulsory stopping place, as it

This page: Sajambre Valley (*Facing page:* Roman Bridge, Cangas de Onís.

is singular for salmon fishing. In the old days, General Franco used to fish in these pools with a local, and spiteful tongues rumour that the fish were previously lured in to ensure the success of the day's fishing. Cement salmon ladders and "landings" follow the whole course of the river and jut out into the pools, where the beaten water forms eddies and cascades of bubbles, the bottom invisible to the eye. The salmon rest or begin their ascent of the river up the ladders, offering a spectacular sight as they jump out of the water in their attempt to fight the current.

The road now takes us more quickly to Cangas de Onís, with its Roman bridge. The town is very stately, with great stone houses that speak of the high-class summer residents of times gone by, second homes and hostels constantly being added to this town where hundreds of tourists gather every Sunday, with Covadonga a stone's throw away.

The site of the old Riaño is now covered by the reservoir - *translator's note.*

FROM OSEJA TO PÍO
I

OSEJA DE SAJAMBRE - VIERDES - PÍO

11 km

Just inside Oseja, a narrow made-up road leads off to the left to Vierdes (2.5 km.) and Pío (3.2 km.). The route begins winding downhill over the narrow asphalt between meadows replete with flowers, butterflies and birds, with a wide variety of trees, ranging from the large and haughty oak and wide-crowned chestnuts to cherry trees, maples, plum trees and hazels. In spring, with its riot of flowers, the area takes on the status of a mountain garden, though it is nice to visit at any time as this little nook enjoys a good climate. The route then goes through a tunnel of vegeta-

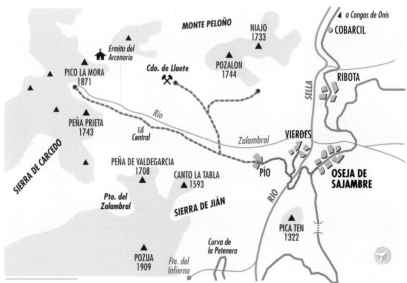

Facing page, top: Peloño Forest, with Mt Jario in the background • *Bottom:* Bringing in the livestock in Sajambre.

tion, which often makes it impossible to enjoy panoramic views. Streams and little gorges are constantly around us. On reaching an unsignposted junction, we turn down to the right towards Vierdes, a small village with renovated and well-preserved houses contrasting with others in ruins. The inhabitants of the village number less than thirty but they are reputed to be the longest-lived in the whole valley, which is attributed to the climate and peace of the area. Ash trees are abundant and there is absolute calm, broken only by birdsong. A path leads off from here along which walkers can reach Ribota, on the Cangas road almost at the beginning of the Los Beyos Canyon. The walk takes an hour between wide meadows crossed by the River Zalambral and with the heights of Mt Niajo (1,733 m.) to our left. This walk is recommended for bird-watchers, as they can observe here the green woodpecker, house martin, crag martin, wren, dunnock, blackcap, Bonelli's warbler, robin, blackbird, thrush, blue tit, great tit and chaffinch, not forgetting the bullfinch, jay and carrion crow. Insects offer great possibilities for close-up photography, which can also be said of the flowers the meadows teem with.

If we want to go to Pío, we turn round and at the first junction we turn right, going up into a landscape similar to the previous one. Pío is not small and has stone houses and smoking chimneys on narrow streets we can easily get lost in, with water flowing from its fountain throughout the year. At the end of the village a track leads off passable for cars we are not too fussy about, but more suitable for 4WDs and mountain bikes. Pío power station is three kilometres away, at the end of a wide valley with Oseja in the background. The river runs fierce through a dense shade of ash, hazel and willow, forming attractive places for photography or rest. Walking from the power station, we can follow the river up to its source, at the foot of the Pico de la Mora, hardly an hour's climb away amid a beautiful landscape of meadows and beechwood, with snow on the summits of the peaks. Roe deer give themselves away with their barking and the tracks of pine martens, genets, weasels and foxes appear on the trail. The loneliness of the area, its absolute peace and the lack of visitors ensure that we are practically alone, isolated from civilization.

On our way to the power station, about halfway up the track, we saw that another one led away to the right, going over to the opposite slope and leading quickly up to the old mine, where there is a view of the pass, where the great fields do not spoil the view of the mountains of Peloño. Instead of going up, you can skirt round the slope following the track that takes you to the mini-reservoir commanding a view of Vierdes and with

Oseja opposite. Bathing is not a good idea because the water is very cold, but the temptation to indulge is great on hot summer days and more than one have tried it (apparently successfully). The slopes are steep and open, with meadows, oaks, ashes and chestnuts. From here, turning round and taking the track down into the valley, we go back again to the village.

Above: Peña Niajo.

FROM VIEGO TO SANTILLÁN
II

VIEGO - BELEÑO - CASONA DE MESTAS -
SELLAÑO - PORCIA - SANTILLÁN

29 km

Well into the Los Beyos Canyon, a little further on from the road tunnel, an asphalt track goes off to the left for Cándano (1 km.), a recommendable detour if we wish to enjoy the Andamios Gorge of the River Porciles. We park the car just outside the village to continue on foot to Viboli (a little over 2 km.) and see the gorge, where the river jumps between the crags and cascades leap from the very limestone and the vegetation makes the air dark, green and damp, and chestnut, hazel and walnut give shade to bilberries and strawberries. The walk there and back takes a little more than an hour, but with frequent stops to take photographs of increasingly surprising nooks and crannies. These are little known routes, or at least they lack the renown of others, but at no moment will the traveller be disappointed by them, rather they will allow him to be alone with the mountain itself.

The route we are going to do begins at the end of the Los Beyos Canyon, where the road to Viego leads off to the left. It is narrow and goes up beside the River Santagustia, which rises on the slopes of Peña Salón (1,243 m.). The meadows are greatly tilted, and chestnuts, service trees and plum trees are abundant. Soon a ravine as narrow as Los Beyos has us sounding the horn at each bend, for in the event of our meeting another vehicle, one of us will have to get out of the way, which is not too easy here.

The river descends in a series of jumps amid moss-covered stones forming little pools barely visible through the gallery forest. The dipper, wren and nightingale have become familiar figures along these paths.

The drive up to the village is difficult, past green meadows whose boundaries follow the contour lines. The old stone houses are well main-

Facing page: The Los Beyos Gorge.

tained, and the implements left outside their doors announce the livestock-rearing vocation of the local people. A few new houses contrast with the old ones, as a tribute to a tourism-based expansion or at least one of holiday rest. The air is heavy with the smell of cows, and a whole undamaged *hórreo* (see p.234), displays its wooden silhouette. With the fruit trees in blossom and the rose bushes blooming, the village acquires an uncustomary liveliness that invites us to take a leisurely stroll around its streets. After the village the road continues endlessly up, coming to a bend with an observation area (with a little bench to sit on) from which we can look out over the whole valley and see the Curezu crests (1,132 m.), with a narrow gorge at the end. Viego is divided into two quarters, upper and lower, not that this causes any rivalry or dispute among its inhabitants. The view is well worth a few photos.

The road keeps climbing, the meadows enclosed with wooden fences until they give way to beech and holly. From the top of the pass (the Llomena Gap) there is a panoramic view of the beechwoods and mountains of Pandemules and Cordal, with Mt Tiatordos (1,951m.) not far away. Right at the top, to the right is a track for the 4WD, which forks after a few metres; to the left is the way to Pico Pierzo (1,552 m.), a good route for walking, as the summit is about 4 km. away over an abrupt and magnificent landscape. The right-hand fork is suitable for the 4WD, which can reach Villaverde, and from there, over asphalt roads, continue towards Porcia.

The downward journey is very steep, with sharp bends and sloping, almost vertical meadows, with the mountains always in the background. Dunnocks, blackcaps, Bonelli's warblers, blue tits, great tits, serins, jays,

Facing page, top: Viego • *bottom:* Panoramic view from Mt Beleño.

carrion crows, wagtails and blackbirds are among the species we may hear and, with a little luck, see and photograph.

A short distance before San Juan de Beleño, the road leads off to Sobrefoz (3.8 km.), where the bends and beech trees try to outnumber each other and bestow an unusual beauty on the scenery.

Beleño is divided into three levels, some houses dominating others in a balcony-like formation overlooking the valley. The new houses and the old are mingled together, which confers size on the village, where the youthful atmosphere is present in every street, affording joy and colour. The peaks and mountains seem to protect it from the elements, and the meadows and market gardens are resplendent in this scenery.

After Beleño, the road goes steeply down, fringed by stout chestnuts, cherry trees, sprouting oaks, willows, service trees and hazels, giving rise to an abundant and varied fauna.

We come to a junction and turn right, following a mountain river, the Ponga, its turbulent waters opening up a path through the narrowness of the gaps in the mountains. The road is now wider and has a good surface.

This page: Panorama from the side of Mt Beleño • *Facing page:* The medicinal great yellow gentian.

Suddenly, after a bend, we come to the Casona de Mestas*, a tourist complex with a spa and rugged surroundings, almost off the beaten track, where the jay and the grey wagtail seem to be permanent tenants and where the traveller is guaranteed peace of mind but without ignoring the delights of Asturian gastronomy. The rock walls are almost vertical, and the dominant vegetation is gorse. The gorge widens and narrows to the rhythm of a river whose flow-rate increases at every step.

Then comes Sellaño, which gives a sensation of smallness, almost nothing but a couple of old houses and in the doorway of one of them an old woman lets enormous columns of smoke away from her cigarette, forming an almost surrealistic and anachronic image. As we go forward, however, the village gets bigger, spreading along the bank of the river, where there are magnificent pools for fishing (if it were not forbidden). Little by little, the landscape widens out into magnificent meadows: the water meadows of Sebarga and Cirieño, which take up the whole valley. We reach Porcia and shortly afterwards come to Santillán, to join the main route, now on the way to Cangas de Onís.

* Or, House of the Mestas. The Mestas were the powerful guilds of shepherds involved in times gone by in transhumance along set routes- *translator's note*

FROM OSEJA DE SAJAMBRE TO VEGABAÑO
III

OSEJA DE SAJAMBRE - SOTO DE SAJAMBRE - VEGABAÑO BYRES -
Cotorra De Escobaño • Senda Del Arcediano • "The Archdeacon's
Path" • Holy Crag (Peña Santa)

11 km

Surely this is one of the prettiest routes in the Picos, something for the car lover to enjoy in a relaxed fashion, but a difficult test for hillwalkers wishing to go on from Vegabaño with their sights set higher, for example on getting a close look at the Holy Crag. The description will be given by stretches, as the possibilities and difficulties are very different, though there is always an outing suitable for the aptitudes of each individual.

We leave Oseja for Cangas, taking the detour to Soto de Sajambre after a very sharp bend. The road is made up but it is very narrow, clim-

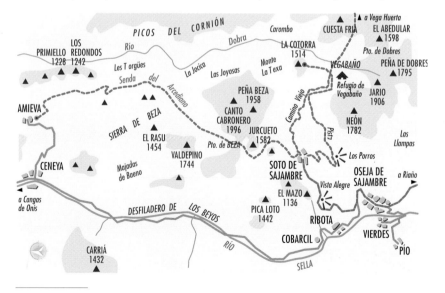

Facing page: Up to Vegabaño on horseback.

bing between the brambles, hazels, ashes and maples waymarking it. After a while we come to the Vistalegre observation area, a great balcony-shaped place opening towards Los Beyos and opposite the Mallet Cross (La Cruz de los Mazos, 1,156 m.), a limestone mass like a natural castle where the River San Pedro leaps over an impressive waterfall. Ribota, Pío and Vierdes appear in the distance, almost from a bird's eye-view. A hundred metres further on, the Picarancón tunnel is the real gateway to the valley, the scenery changing radically, now one of green meadows, some flat and others on the sloping mountain sides, fringed by trees, following the River Agüera, which has a small dam. This heavenly nook, with the beechwood so near we can almost feel it, is home to a varied fauna - fox, wild cat, weasel, wild boar, pine marten, carrion crow, jay, bullfinch, serin, chaffinch, nuthatch, coal tit, robin, Bonelli's warbler, wren - as well as countless insects and flowers that are a delight for the photographer.

At the end of the valley is Soto de Sajambre, the meeting point for tra-vellers who stroll up and down its narrow streets impressed by wooden galleries, the doors of the houses, the stacks of firewood awaiting the

This page: Sajambre Valley • *Facing page:* Soto de Sajambre, with Peña Beza in the background.

harsh winter to warm the homes, clogs clacking over the ground, cowbells whose wearers block the streets with their lazy gait, and the *hórreos* (see p. 234) which seem to keep a thousand secrets. It is the departure point for more daring enterprises; in the bar we hear conversations about the Perro Gully, the fog or the rain that doesn't ease up all week, the bear that has been sighted near the byre or the dreaded presence of the wolf, which causes the guard to be doubled over the livestock. These chats serve as a sort of psychological preparation for the less decided, helped by a coffee with a goodly amount of *orujo* (see p. 239) in it, which washes our cares away in an instant.

From Soto to the byres at Vegabaño there is a track for 4WDs, but many other cars manage to climb the six kilometres between the two points. If the final destination is the meadows or the refuge at Vegabaño, it is a good idea to walk, and, what's more, along the Camino Viejo ("Old Path"), a track with a continuous climb but no great vertical difference, allowing us to enjoy typical beechwood scenery. The trees stand like great

Following double page: Vegabaño byres *(left)*. *Hórreo* at Soto de Sajambre *(top right)* and horses *(bottom right)*.

51

masts loaded with branches affording shade to an undergrowth which is not too dense and where the bilberry is plentiful. The trees filter and sieve the light into amazing colours and shapes and the stillness of the air is only disturbed by birdsong or by the breeze moving the leaves. Foggy days are the other side of the trip, when we try to pick out the track (you can't miss it) among the unreal shapes of the thick trunks, almost erased from a minimal but evocative landscape, where the individual imagination may play with absolute freedom. Birdlife is important here, and

among it is the famous capercaillie, with a sparse but stable population in the Cantabrian Mountains. Occasionally to be seen also is the brown bear, having a siesta at the beginning of winter in sight of the village.

After five sharp bends (of the wide track), a path leads off in front of us which takes us over the thirty metres to the Porros observation area, which is perhaps too little known among visitors. The are two stone tables with sturdy benches there where we can eat unhurriedly. All of the Sajambre Valley lies before us, a view difficult to forget.

Nearly at the end of the track, a barrier will not let the car through. We leave it in an improvised parking space to come suddenly into the *Majada* (=byre area, see note on p. 64) of Vegabaño, a large area of sparse pastureland criss-crossed by tiny streams that flood the land, springs appearing hear and there allowing us to take on fresh water. Almost at the end of the meadow is the refuge, with abundant information and the possibility of meeting guides for the following day's outings. Camping is allowed and tents often outnumber the flowers in summer, giving rise to new relationships and nocturnal chats that last almost until daybreak.

Facing page: Winter in Soto de Sajambre • *This page:* Vegabaño, with the Holy Crag in the background.

From here there are several different outings for the hillwalker, depending on how far he feels like walking and how much time he has.

Cotorra de Escobaño (1,528 m.)
The path starts at the top, going up 250 m. to the left through the beechwood, where the holly bushes keep their dark green colour all the year round. The summit can be reached in an hour, with a view of the highest peaks of this massif. If we keep going along the path we can get to Amieva, walking along the River Dobra for much of the way and going past Carombo to the Jocica dam. The path goes down 700 m. in 12 km., so we need five hours to enjoy the scenery, which constantly changes. The

walk back is rather tiring on the legs, but we can always get one of the group to pick us up at Amieva or Ceneya.

The Archdeacon's Path (Soto-Amieva)

This is surely one of the best known routes for those who love to wear out boots and enjoy scenery. No great effort is necessary, but some preparation is needed to walk for seven hours over land that doesn't stop surprising us with breathtaking views or tiny details, such as the delicate-

Facing page, top: View from the Cotorra de Escobaño (*Bottom:* the River Dobra • *Below:* The Archdeacon's Path.

looking houseleeks clinging to the rocks, the acrobatic flight of the chough, the roe-deer, and a thousand other little things of a privileged fauna and flora.

What is now a track used to be the main artery of communication between these two villages, so any local shepherd can give us a unique description of the route. It was opened thanks to a great man, Pedro Díaz (17th Century), a man of great personal wealth and a benefactor who gave the Sajambre Valley culture and opened it up to the world.

The path starts in Soto de Sajambre itself and follows the Culabragañas brook between meadows and trees (willows, ashes, hazels), to go on up to the Beza Pass, past the peak of Mt Jurcueto (1,590 m.) on the left. The pass marks the border between the provinces of León and Asturias, although the paths and valleys are ignorant of such distinctions and the scenery is a continuous whole. The downward journey is gentle, taking us to the Toneyo byres, with stone refuges, low with narrow doors to keep the cold out. A little lower down we come to the Toneyo stream, which gives its name to the valley. The pastures are of sparse but dense clumps as far up as Valdepino (1,744 m.). We then keep on down to where the valley is wider and the grass is longer and there is livestock to benefit from it.

A little over half way, at a bend in the path, we go past the Les Torgües spring on the right, where we may well stop and regain strength while we enjoy the cool clean water. To the right we see the impressive limestone of the Ordiales, with snow still on the crests and clouds tangled round the peaks, with heath and broom on the slopes. On this route, loneliness and the immensity of the mountains make themselves felt, as do the change from one valley to another, the harshness of the climate, the verticalness of the limestone and the gentleness of the pastures. A smooth climb takes us up to Les Texuques (1,058 m.) and a view of the Amieva Valley, where meadows are again the chief constituent of the scenery, livestock rearing is the mainstay of wealth and the friendliness of the people is the main characteristic of the area.

To the bottom of the Holy Crag

We return to a traditional route for those who wish to reach the bottom of the Holy Crag, enjoy a varied scenery and brag of having beaten the Perro ("Dog") Gully to conquer the panoramic view from the Burro

---

Facing page, top: Soto de Sajambre and the Beza Massif • *Bottom:* Beza Massif.

("Donkey") Gap. It's not an easy thing to do, but nothing is impossible for those with willpower and...the whole day before them (about 6 hours is enough for the journey, allowing for frequent stops).

This new route allows us to enjoy two clearly different landscapes. On the one hand is the valley, lying on limestones, slates and quartzite, with a well developed soil supporting mainly hayfields, the result of human settlement. On the other hand is the high mountain scenery, formed from limestone deposits which have undergone severe erosion to form unrepeatable shapes. Rocky outcrops are frequent, making progress difficult but making the mountainside beautiful.

We set out form the Vegabaño byres taking the path leading away from the end of the refuge (any doubt may be resolved here and now, either from the explanations of the guides or from the maps papering the walls), to go into the beechwood after enjoying the idyllic backwaters created by clean-water streams like the River Truégano, the Riega Seca and the Riega Grande. Holly bushes are widely spaced and the wood is sufficiently big to be worth a good look. Buzzards fly over the trees, broom and meadows which we shall soon come to. Here, the capercaillie has an excellent place for his spring courtship, so extreme care and silence must be unbreakable rules of conduct. From any tree, a wood pigeon may fly noisily out - they have made us jump more than once. The wren, dunnock, blackcap, goldcrest, black redstart, robin, song thrush, blue tit, great tit, nuthatch,

Facing page: Sajambre Woods. The *Roblón* (Great Oak), quite a symbol of eternity.

jay, chaffinch, greenfinch, lizard, pine marten, beech marten, fox, wolf, weasel, dormouse, little owl and barn owl, from an almost endless list, are habitual fellow-travellers; you just have to know how to listen and keep your eyes open.

You will soon come to the *Roblón*, an enormous oak tree six feet across, famous among all hillwalkers. The path goes near it, in the Salambre forest, open, easy to walk in, if you want to get off the track. Beech trees leave the ground clean, where bilberries, junipers and other plants form a thick carpet rather than an obstacle to the walker.

We turn to the left to go past the Salambre Peak and reach the Frade Top. From here, a track goes off to the right, which we leave to come to a

Above: Dusk in the Holy Crag Massif.

fork and take the left branch. The waymarks and signs left by other mountaineers keep us on the track and we don't lose our way. We are surrounded by high challenging crags, but the Perro Gully is a great temptation, and it is before us. We zigzag up, tripping over stones and puffing on the slopes, but little by little we overcome the difficulty and reach the Donkey Gap, a narrow passage between the limestone heights with views of the Holy Crag. A rest is almost compulsory and certainly well earned.

The griffon vulture flies over our heads at a great height, while the wallcreeper is almost at our side; present also are the linnet, the alpine chough and the snow-finch, depending on the time of year we choose for our outing. The views are breathtaking as we are surrounded by almost naked crags, hardly bearing lichens. We are protected by Picos del Verde

(2,179 m.), Mt Moledizos (2,233 m.), Mt Cuetalbo (2,163 m.) and, in front of us, Torres de Cotalbín (2,193 m.).

The descent isn't difficult and lets us admire the landscape. Then comes another climb before we go down again to Vega Huerta (2,100 m.), where there is a small refuge and many marks left by tents. A fountain allows us to take on water or to prepare a meal, our main concern once we have reached this point. We are at the very feet of the Holy Crag (2,596 m.), the highest summit around here, gazing at the south face of this colossus where the snow lasts all year and whose crests look like the walls of some gigantic castle, and the invitation to climb is an almost irresistible temptation.

If we still have any strength or sense of excitement left, we can complete the route by going right down to the River Cares, a walk lasting about three hours down the Capozo Gully. For this we take the track off to the right, a slight climb up to see the Cabronal scree and then down and down until we get to the byres of the same name. The descent is steeper as far as Verón del Corbo, then becoming a zigzag stairway down to the Yedra cave, to gentle out at Las Cavidas and divert to the side of La Farfada. From here, the easiest way is via the El Tombo observation area, as we follow the contour round and hardly make any effort on this last stretch. On the other side of the river, Cordiñanes comes into sight, where we'll be able to find everything necessary to get our energy back after our effort or to spend the night and work out a route for the next day.

From Vegabaño, there are many other routes, too many to mention. If you are willing to live your own adventures, ask the shepherds first to find out about any likely route and don't forget to add another hour to the time they consider necessary to do it, just in case, as they are used to the tracks and for them the slopes just don't seem to exist.

---

* There are many references to byres throughout this book. These are not only used by livestock but also by their keepers, as livestock rearing is not carried on here on farms as such, but on common land - *translator's note.*

Facing page, top: Towards the Frade Top • *Bottom:* Vega Huerta.

FROM CANGAS DE ONÍS TO THE LAKES
IV

CANGAS DE ONÍS - COVADONGA - MIRADOR DE LA REINA ("QUEEN'S OBSERVATION AREA") -LES VALERES COL - LAKE LA ERCINA - LAKE ENOL

21 km

We leave Cangas at dawn, with a fine mist that makes the silent scenery of the sleeping town damp. New buildings, hotels and houses appear before us as we advance along a road with impeccable asphalt, amid meadows of long grass, disperse trees, gentle bends. We come to the junction to turn towards Covadonga, following the river of the same name. The road is good and the scenery varied in an area given over to a summer tourism that invades every corner.

From the Royal Site (see p. 239), the road to the Lakes leads off to the left, already climbing, under a tunnel of trees that play with the light. The sun is in front of us and silhouettes take over from solid bodies. We begin a spectacular climb, gaining height and leaving the beechwoods and great ash trees behind us. Limestone dominates the scenery, the road gets narrower and steep sloping bends come one after another.

The Queen's Observation Area (Mirador de la Reina), hard up against the asphalt, is our first stop. There is a very wide panoramic view, but the sea of cloud lets the peaks show and hides the valleys. When it breaks up, the meadow of Gamonedo and Sojaedo appears green and vigorous, with the Güeña Valley in the background and the heights of Cardosas, Cuesta Cavia and Cabeza Severa before us. In this way the crags combine with the meadows, the patches of woodland and disperse hamlets. We keep on up, accompanied all the way by the limestone and the pastures that change positions at each bend, until we get to the Pellín Height, between the Peña del Elefante ("Elephant Crag" - you can make out the head and trunk) and Canto Fuerte; needle furze and gorse mix with heather and the dwarf junipers that cover the ground, poking out of every gap in the rock with a contrast of colours. At last we are at the Les Veleres Col, at the foot of the

---

Facing page, top: Lake Enol • *Bottom:* Lake La Ercina.

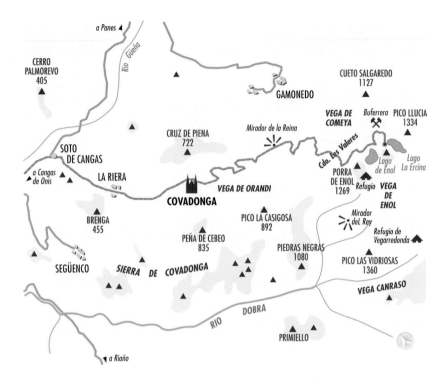

Porra de Enol ("Enol Knoll"), with Lake Enol below us. At this col there is a monument to José Ramón Lueje, with the Cornión Peaks in the background, still with snow on their summits.

Lake Enol is almost circular, with blue water reflecting a clear sky over its 12 hectares of area. The depth of this glacial lake is about 25 metres and in the deepest part lies a figure of Our Lady of Covadonga, taken down there by a group of divers from Gijón. Trout and crayfish abound, while on the surface, a few coots and mallards leave their wakes on the water. The road goes round the edge of the lake until it reaches its highest point, where there is a junction. Turning right and going up, we come to a wide flat area where a large hotel is being built. A wide earth track takes us 300 metres further to the Mirador del Príncipe ("Prince's Observation Area"). It is a circular construction of limestone and cement with a rather narrow way in. Once inside, explanations on panels tell us how a lake disappeared and became the Comeya meadow. The view is fantastic, over an enormous hollow turned pasture, where a couple of streams keep the grass growing and livestock abounds, the sound of their bells reaching the

observation area. We are looking into the disused iron and magnesium mine, surrounded by a limestone cirque protecting the meadow, and behind us are the heights of the Holy Crag. The dark colour of a few tiles contrasts with the whitish hue of the limestone, and the slopes are dotted with beeches.

We go down from the observation area to approach Lake La Ercina, also glacial, which is long and shallow (maximum depth 3 metres), which allows for the growth of a marsh-type vegetation which shelters coots, mallards, teal, moorhens, pochards, snipes and the odd heron, depending on the time of year we go there. Ravens, griffon vultures and Egyptian vultures come flying over the peaks. This lake has a car park which into summer is not big enough and which is the starting point for several outings in the National Park, like the route to the Ario refuge (3-4 hours), over limestone, cols and gullies, all the while walking through mountain scenery.

Above: Queen's Observation Area.

If we go back to the beginning, at the Les Veleres Col a track leads off (cars can go down it) which goes round Lake Enol and into the meadow, where there are places marked for camping and which is an ideal place to spend a few days. So begins the route proposed for acquainting us with such an immense and varied landscape.

Above: The privileged setting of the Covadonga Basilica.

TO THE ORDIALES OBSERVATION AREA
V

LAKE ENOL - MIRADOR DEL REY ("KING'S OBSERVATION AREA") - VEGARREDONDA - ORDIALES OBSERVATION AREA

8 km

It is possible to go from the lake to the King's Observation Area by car, though the walk is worth the effort, as the land is practically flat on the Enol meadow, where there are pastures with beautifully kept sheds and winter byres, and livestock that grazes without a care in the world. The flow of tourists is high, and one unwinds gazing at mountains, butterflies, lizards, redstarts, choughs and pretty girls.

The King's Observation Area overlooks the gorge of the River Pomperi, with the Pico de las Vidriosas on the left and Piedras Negras ("Black Stones") opposite. Below us is a spread of beechwood with service trees,

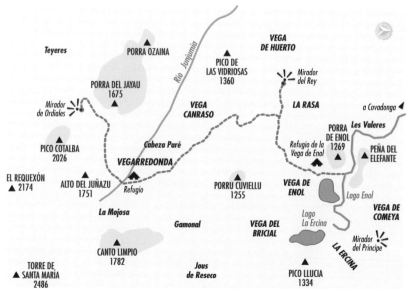

limes, holly, and some oak and birch in the upper part. It is a good hide-out for the capercaillie, and the woodcock may be seen and heard when the promise of dawn is as yet unfulfilled. Beside us, the wheatear is nervous of our presence.

From the observation area, the path for cars goes about 500 metres, and comes to an end, where we have to put our boots on if we wish to continue. The track is wide, and goes past a fountain and picnic area, where the climb up the Vega Espino ("Hawthorn Meadow") begins. Steep slopes are in sight, but meadows and livestock abound, as do winter byres, tourists and choughs. The path gets narrower bit by bit and sometimes disappears, but it can easily be found again (by following the yellow marks). After an hour and a half we come to the Vegarredonda refuge, a circle of limestone and snow, where grass, moss, lichens, heather and hawthorns grow sheltered.

From here there is a pretty climb up to the Ordiales observation area, which can be done easily in an hour and a half. At the beginning the ascent is steep, up a well-marked track past the strange figures eroded from the rock, small snowfields, narrow valleys, sheer limestone faces, streams and screes. We soon come to the Ordiales field, where there is a refuge owned by ICONA*, with the door open. To get to the top of the field means a good climb up the pasture, a short rest and a final effort to climb the last few metres, frankly very steep, with loose stones, treading a zigzag path.

The reward for our effort is wonderful. We are in the observation area, next to the tomb of Don Pedro Pidal, who has rested under such a privileged balcony since 1949 at his own wish and thanks to the efforts of the hillwalkers.

A sheer drop of a thousand metres is almost the first thing we see. Then, after we recover, the panorama before us is immense, with the Dobra Valley at our feet, myriad peaks all around, with the Torre Santa ("Holy Tower") nearby and the Canto Cabronero not far away, patches of woodland dotted over valleys and slopes, great and small gorges, vertical peaks, gaps, intricate patterns of light and shade, fog and cloud, and right by us, less than ten metres away, a pair of choughs in their courtship flight, then perching on an arête over the drop.

We don't notice the passage of time as we are engrossed in the scenery of the Picos de Europa, dreaming of new routes and climbs, but

---

Preceding double page: Prince's Observation Area *(left).* Ordiales *(top right).* Vegarredonda *(middle right).* The way to Ordiales *(bottom right).*

above all, enjoying a moment that will never be repeated, for if we return a thousand times, on each occasion we shall observe new aspects and sensations of the landscape.

* ICONA (Instituto Nacional de la Conservación de la Naturaleza) = National Nature Conservancy Institute - *translator's note*.

Above: From the Ordiales Observation Area, the Picos seem infinite.

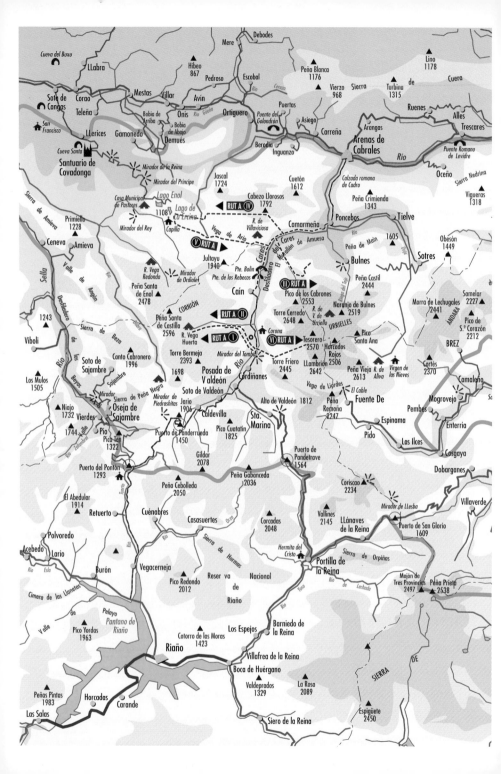

THE WATERS OF THE CARES

Three

RIAÑO - PONTÓN PASS - PANDERRUEDAS PASS - CALDEVILLA -
SOTO DE VALDEÓN - POSADA DE VALDEÓN - CORDIÑANES -
CAÍN - CAMARMEÑA - ARENAS DE CABRALES

53 km

This route may be attacked from Panes in Cantabria, Cangas de Onís in Asturias or Riaño in León. For the sake of continuity with the previous section, we shall start the description at Riaño and later we'll take it from the other points mentioned.

Leaving Riaño we take the road to the Pontón Pass, a stretch we already know. A little beyond the wayside chapel off to the right is the junction with the road to the Paderruedas Pass up the narrow River Tuerto towards its source. There is no shortage of meadows but the dominant scenery is an unbroken beechwood stretching from the river's edge to the summits. The road climbs gently showing the hues of the leaves changing with the seasons, autumn being the most suggestively picturesque time. A great bend leaves the Llavaris Col to our left, a steep beech-covered slope where it is difficult to keep one's balance because of the lie of the land and the dampness of the ground. Here roe-deer are abundant, as are other species, outstanding among which are the black woodpecker and, surely, the capercaillie. To the right is a vast field and at the roadside itself is a privileged spot from which to observe chamois and roe-deer grazing. The meadow borders the beechwood on the Los Carros

Ridge, at the end of which is Mt Los Hoyos (1,865 m.) and the Frañana Gap, the source of the River Cares, though some consider it to rise at the Panderruedas Gap itself. There are one or two tracks in the area, but their use is not recommended as the area is of great ecological importance and its balance is somewhat delicate, so deciding against going down these paths is a step in the right direction towards preserving this spot.

Our reward is nigh, however, for the Paderruedas Pass (1,450 m.) is at hand. Just before reaching the top, we have a panoramic view of the Sajambre Valley, and in the flattish area around the top we suddenly see the Picos limestone. To the left is a track which takes us relaxingly up to the Piedrashitas observation area. The traditional bet of the last one to get there paying for the coffee causes the car to be hurriedly vacated. It's only ten minutes through beechwood to stand on a modernist cement balcony, which contrasts with the rest of the landscape. A sort of metal sculpture there is interpreted by the forest rangers as a "wind flute", as it produces strange sounds on windy days. From here our gaze is greeted by the vast bulk of Torre Bermeja, Torre Cerredo, Mt Llambrión and Peñas Cifuentes, with the beechwood in the foreground where the dark green of the holly is noticeable. To the left is the Pico de las Guadañas ("Scythes Peak", 1,767 m.), prominent for the beechwood crowning its crest, and which alone makes a fine outing. To the left is the Pico de Cuatatín (1,682 m.), and the whole valley ahead. Back at the car we find the doors closed and the keys in full view inside. After several attempts to break in...the spare keys appear, and what could have ruined our day out is no more than a passing shock.

The road down from the pass is very steep, beech trees around us all the way, with bends that strain the driver's attention down to the Valdeón observation area, a perfect name, as it dominates the whole width of the valley. The villages look like tiny fairy houses set in wide green meadows. Most of the scenery is taken up by beechwood and the holly patches are now very noticeable, as they form dense thickets that give shelter to a great many animals on windy and cold winter days.

Preceding double page: Valdeón Valley, Central Massif (Mts Palanca, Llambrión and Friero stand out).

As we go down, the scenery becomes tamer and our attention is centred on the hayfields, some flat, others almost vertical, all of them populated in spring with flowers and insects that delight the amateur naturalist; irises are plentiful, with their intense blue colour; clovers, mallows, geraniums and pimpernels give a special colouring to these fields, which are fertilized and mown in spring. The first village we come to is Caldevilla, just off the road. It is typical in its appearance and traditions of the mountain region, with stone houses, red roofs and wooden galleries twisted by the course of time. Its mainstay is livestock breeding, though in summer, tourism transforms the atmosphere and takes up all the spare beds. Next door is Soto de Valdeón, which is bigger, with a camp site which also fills up with visitors, on the banks of a River Cares which has already increased its flow-rate. From here walks can be organized to Vegabaño and Torre Bermeja, fairly easy to get to, and any local will give you accurate directions (though it's more than a good idea to take a guide book).

THE DIVINE GORGE. POSADA DE VALDEÓN - PONCEBOS

18 km

Accompanied by cherry trees in blossom we go down into an ever-widening valley to Posada de Valdeón, the real beginning of the route. Posada has changed a lot in the last few years, with new houses added to the old ones, and a much larger number of places to stay for a burgeoning tourist trade that is truly massive in the summer months. Nevertheless, it has demonstrated an ability to retain rural tradition and culture, and the tourist must visit the great lime tree in the main square and buy a few cheeses from the nearby factory. An asphalt path leaves Posada that a car can go along, but running into serious trouble in the event of meeting one coming the other way. This road would take us to Caín itself, but the long walk is worth the effort, for

Following double page: Posada de Valdeón *(top left).* Soto de Valdeón *(bottom left).* Crown Chapel *(top right).* Caín *(bottom right).*

this way we'll be able to take in the full greatness of the landscape.

A short distance away is Los Llanos, overlooking the banks of the Cares, now with a more than sufficient flow, and where the evenings bring unique light-patterns of shapes and colours. It's a very special light, which has to be enjoyed.

Cordiñanes is at the end, on the right bank, small, livestock-based and a tourist centre, with cement streets and a trade in local woodcraft, walking sticks and staves being excellent purchases for the wayfarer and a help in avoiding falls on the paths. After the village there is a steep slope down to the river, which we must cross to get to the mythical El Tombo observation area (for car lovers, there is good asphalt to take us to it quickly). There is a statue of a chamois, the emblematic animal of the area, standing on this balcony open to surprises, where there is graphic information concerning the peaks surrounding us. Torre del Friero (2,445 m), Torre de la Palanca (2,614 m.) and Mt Llambrión (2,642 m.) are among the limestone colossi standing before us. The succession of crests, high plateaux, cols, gullies and overhangs is continuous. At first we want to see everything at once, as though we did not have enough time to look at so many things. We then calm down and enjoy each part in turn, the sun and clouds changing the scenery by moments, and fog is sometimes an unwelcome visitor, although its presence creates a difference ambience, another world.

From the observation area, a steep descent takes us down through a very tunnel of vegetation. The beeches, oaks, walnuts, hazels, limes and ashes insist on strangling the narrow road, while a long repertoire of fauna appears before our eyes. By the stones, an Iberian rock lizard looks small beside a green lizard, quick as a flash at running away as we approach to take the requisite photo. A dipper flies in a straight line above the river and a wren flies away before our feet. This is a walk for frequent stops to close our eyes and discover the world of sounds that bring us new sensations in another way of enjoying nature which is too often forgotten.

Facing page: Posada de Valdeón.
Following double page: La Peguera *(top left).* The *Chorco* (Wolf trap) *(bottom left).* El Tombo Observation Area *(right).*

We go by the Corona stream and the mountain of the same name, recognizable from its diverse vegetation. The winter byres beside us are wonderfully preserved and the sheep are dispersed in groups on the meadows we leave behind us, until we come to a strange structure: the *Chorco de los Lobos* (wolf trap), an ingenious device for catching the wolves that used to come to the area and could decimate the flocks

Then we come to the River Peguera, which rises in the shadow of Torres de Cotalbín (2,193 m.), crossed by the Capozo bridge amid wide meadows contrasting with the nearby summits. As we go forward, we approach a Cares that begins to get strangled by a gorge with vertical sides, a foretaste of the so-called Divine Gorge, which we shall find after Caín. We are between the Torre de Comea (1,588 m.) to the left and the Peñas de Padrún on the other side. The water of the Cares now leaps between the crags, incapable of silencing the noise produced by a waterfall at the end of the path, right by the Reguera bridge. It is the anteroom of Caín, which soon appears before us.

Caín consists of two parts, the Lower one, the beginning of the walk through the gorge, and the Upper one, more withdrawn into the shade of Mt Moñero and Mt Cardeda, and much less well known. The houses are of traditional stone construction, with a square groundplan and two storeys, although new buildings with different designs are taking their places alongside them.

The route goes along the river and is only for boots (although some mountain bikes venture along it) and will take us to the very heart of the mountains. We cross by the Pinteros bridge and come to the little dam of the power station (Electra de Viesgo) to continue alongside the canal, which is always full of water.

The scenery changes completely. The sides come so close together that tunnels had to be hewn in the limestone. They are not very high and some walkers have to bow their heads to get through, but the windows overlooking the river let us enjoy the

Facing page: Caín.
Following double page: Cares Gorge (left). Narrowing (top right). Bridge over the Cares (bottom right).

spectacle of the gorge. The mountains become vertical to reach the sky, almost out of eyesight; the beech trees grow in unlikely gaps with twisted trunks almost stuck to the rock or hanging in an endless void, and the occasional laurel tinges the air dark green. Only the black redstart and the crag martin dare to fly in such a limited space, while the raven and the griffon vulture are the masters of the peaks. The Cares, with its green waters, forms pools and torrents that invite one to rest. For those who want to walk along the riverside itself, there is a minimal track that goes up and down with the obstacles and the lie of the land. It takes a lot of effort, but it gives us a very different view of the gorge.

Shortly afterwards we come to the Trascámara bridge, which crosses the abyss over the river. The sight is unique, with water seeping from every crack, rock faces colonized by moss, vertical lines seemingly drawn with a pen and down below, the river eating out a path and eroding the limestone. If this scenery is awe-inspiring, then reaching the Trea bridge increases the feeling, as the sensation of oppression is so real, and more than one worthy has been overcome by vertigo. Here a well-known route starts up the Trea Gully, but that is for later. Another bridge, Bolín, near the previous one, takes us on to a less narrow gorge but a more spectacular one, as we now have a visual field that allows us to take in the colossal limestone mounds. The Los Papos bridge is near to the León provincial boundary (in the Párvulas Gully) the route continuing into Asturias.

In summer there is a great procession of visitors, queues not being infrequent on the difficult stretches, which gives us the opportunity to make conversation and indeed to bump into a neighbour. So, coming round one of the bends, a marvel appears before us; it's Merche, the nursing auxiliary, who has changed her white coat for tight jeans and a rucksack. Well, let's turn our attention again to the "other" nature.

The first place to appear is Culiembro, worthy of mention for its walnut tree, which offers shade to summer fatigue, and just two winter byres where the shepherds and goatherds spend long days looking after their charges. The continual presence of this

---

Preceding double page: Great Wall of Amuesa *(left).* La Jaya Bridge *(right).*

livestock makes ticks common and easy to catch when we stop. We start nattering to a shepherd, tanned almost black by the sun and the wind, thin as a rake and agile as a goat, whom we ask about one of the possible routes and the possibility of reaching the Lakes of Covadonga from here. The answer, though to be expected, does not fail to be symptomatic of the mountain character: "You can, but there are slopes for running and others for resting..."

Our journey now hits on a very steep slope, in a more open but no less rugged landscape. The passing of thousands of boots cannot avoid loose stones and the odd trip has our fellows colouring their language, as some feet are already pulverized because of unsuitable footwear. After the climb, we are atop Los Collados enjoying the view of the Murallón de Amuesa ("Great Wall of Amuesa"), limestone and more limestone in a variety of shapes and considerable heights. Then, a no less pronounced downward slope takes us to Puente Poncebos, the end of a stony walk and where an asphalt road takes us six kilometres to Arenas de Cabrales, a tourist spot *par excellence* where we find suggestions for new adventures, from horse riding to sailing down the river in a boat. The famous Cabrales, or green, cheese is a must to taste, with its pungent flavour if ever there was one, but which can be combated with a drop of *orujo** with honey.

We suppose you know the old trick of the two cars, one parked at Poncebos and the other at Caín. Half-way along the route the drivers swap keys, the day is not so long, and the reward of a good meal and a long after-dinner chat becomes a reality. All there is left to do is agree on a restaurant, inn or dive to meet in.

* See page 239.

TO LA FARFADA FROM EL TOMBO
I

EL TOMBO OBSERVATION AREA - LA FARFADA SPRING - CAPOZO BRIDGE - CUESTA DEL HOMBRO (SHOULDER HILL) - CHORCO (WOLF TRAP) - EL TOMBO

4 km

This route begins right at the El Tombo observation area. Though not very well known, it will take us to one of the most peaceful and pictures-que places in these mountains. To the left, a wide path leads away over a slope in an open landscape with the limestone preceding Pico Sardón, also to our left. We can't use the 4WD as the path becomes a mere track a hundred metres further on. The gorse combines with a disperse tree cover permitting the presence of pasture, where it is not rare to sight the odd chamois grazing before it flees from sight, although its curiosity will cause it to keep stopping, giving rise to a reciprocal contemplation. The

Facing page: The River Peguera amid luxuriant vegetation.

track is occasionally blocked by plum trees and those careless enough to go in shorts will suffer the odd scratch. Then, bit by bit, the vegetation closes in, giving way to a beechwood whose enormous trees filter the sunlight with their dense branches to provide the necessary shade and humidity for ferns to sprout in every crevice. The stones are covered in moss, and hart's tongue is plentiful. In this semi-darkness the forest floor is like a carpet owing to the bilberry, which covers stone and soil alike and generously offers us its fruit. So we must be careful as we walk, not like Meli, who started to walk backwards to take the photo of her lifetime only to end up being photographed herself in a rather comical pose, to say nothing of the state of her trousers and shirt.

The way is almost flat, with some unevenness that poses no problems. A gentle downward slope takes us to a wooden bridge crossing the river. Just over the bridge a path goes up to the left by the riverside. The river leaps between the stones on its bed creating hundreds of little white cascades of beaten and oxygenated water. Little by little the river bed

Above: La Farfada.

narrows and two hundred metres further up we find its source. From the rock there springs a transparent water forming a small pool set in the shade, announcing an underground river that sees the light of day here for the first time. It is the La Farfada spring, sheltered, surrounded by crags with snow on their summits, with water slipping over their limestone walls, with trees on the steep slopes and above all, the silence of a world of stone. To lie down on our backs and contemplate the rocks and clouds is a pleasure that can take up hours of our time, while we forget our daily lives and raise our spirits in search of higher goals.

We can either go back the way we came or a different way, fairly convenient as it is downhill all the way to the Capozo Bridge. So we go back to the wooden bridge and follow the path we left before. We soon come to an open space, a mountain pasture with heather, juniper, gorse and flowers, abundant in butterflies that distract us with their fluttering. Here the path cuts across the slope and takes us into an area covered by a scree where there are enormous beeches, mixed with rowans, ashes and limes. Sometimes the path disappears from sight, but our intuition takes us back to it. We go over Mt Tras los Redondos to look for the River Peguera. Having got to it, we have two alternatives: the first is to cross over to the other side and follow it over the green fields that surround it. The field boundaries are stone walls and a few beeches shade the pastures where sheep abound, agile and well fed, their wool clean from rubbing between broom and heather. Some scattered winter byres facilitate contact with the shepherds, a situation which must never be overlooked in order to understand their culture and traditions as well as to listen to explanations they will give us about the mountains, the summary of a lifetime in these parts.

The other option (a walk of 9.5 km, all told) is to go upstream on the right-hand side and follow a narrow path that will take us up to the crags. After a vertical difference of 150 metres, which in places leaves us out of breath, we soon come to a nook worthy of a film. It is a sort of natural yard, where a cave, called Lluques, suggests mystical apparitions or affords safe shelter in bad weather. At its feet there is a stream, with, waiting in ambush for it, willow, ash and hazel, sheltering a varied fauna and where birdsong is constant, from the drilling of the woodpecker to the squawking of the jay or the sounds of the great tit, blue tit, short-toed tree-creeper and chaffinch. Beeches, always present, give way to the abundant hazels of straight branches and varying thickness, where the

temptation to make oneself a staff or a stick is great, although we'll find an abundant supply of dry branches perfectly suited to this. As we go up, the wood becomes less dense, the trees get shorter and we come to a compact clump of walnuts. We are on Shoulder Hill, at the feet of Mt Cerra de Cuba (1,961 m.). The view looking towards Torre Cerredo is awe-inspiring, from an angle that is not too well known among visitors and which is certainly worth the effort. At this altitude the last redoubts of snow last until the beginning of the summer. Chamois are easy to see, as

are, in the wood, the rootings of wild boar and the excrement of foxes, weasels, pine martens and beech martens.

The way back to the observation area is along the river, to the Capozo Bridge and then by road to the *Chorco* to begin the hard climb up to El Tombo. If one of our number brings the car down here, the wait will be relaxing and the legs will come in for less punishment.

Above: Descent from La Farfada spring. One of the most beautiful spots in the Picos.

FROM EL TOMBO TO VEGA HUERTA
II

EL TOMBO OBSERVATION AREA - LOS CABIDOS - CAPOZO GULLY - VERÓN DEL CORBO - VEGA HUERTA

10 km

This route should be done the other way round, as that way it would be downhill all the way, the effort would be less and the time needed would be cut right down. So this information should be read both ways, from the beginning and from the end, depending on how the outing has been planned. We must not forget that hillwalking is a very personal thing, each of us knowing his own preferences and limitations. On some

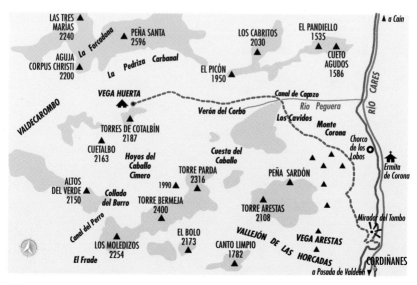

Facing page: Capozo Gully.

walks I have met people who prefer walking up to walking down, and others who like the opposite, as it depends on one's physical fitness and above all one's individual sense of difficulty or danger.

From the El Tombo observation area, we take (or we emerge from) the track leading off to the left, towards the already known La Farfada. We go over the open slope and penetrate into the beechwood, thus reaching the little wooden bridge almost without effort. We continue forwards past La Farfada on our left, leaving Mt Corona to come to a plateau with a good view over the landscape. Then we come to Los Cabidos, with the River Peguera in the background. Then a steep zigzag climb begins. The track, well marked, is covered with little stones that are apt to make us slip. We walk along a sort of cornice cut from the rock, but soon we go into a small beech copse, where we can have our first rest. We gain height quickly, partly using the track and partly up steps hewn from the crag. All this effort takes us to near the Cueva de la Yedra, or Cueva del Agua ("Ivy, or Water Cave"), where the spring is like a blessing on hot days. After another rest, we start up the Capozo Gully, to keep on up till we get to Verón del Corbo, where we have to cross the river to keep climbing to the Cabronal scree*, which lives up to its name and adds difficulty to the route. The worst is now over, and now we can see Vega Huerta from a hillock.

Naturally, from the refuge we can reach Vegabaño via the Donkey Gap if our intention is to go down to Soto de Sajambre.

The walk the other way takes about four hours, and the scenery is worth the effort at every moment, as the proximity of the Holy Crag with its 2,596 m. decrees a greyish limestone landscape with snow dotted on the crests. The air is cold and the wind sometimes blows with quite a force, while on calm and sunny days, the sun seems bent on lacerating us with its rays. The cracks in the limestone shelter houseleeks, harebell, Cantabrian thrift and spring gentian, a whole tiny world of plants capable of living in extreme climatic conditions and that have to flower in a short period of time. Where the soil is thicker, dwarf junipers take over the surface, covering the stones with their rough branches. As you will have supposed, on this route there is an animal that has become the symbol of the region, the chamois, in small groups grazing on vertical mountain sides, how it keeps its balance being completely beyond us, or fleeing from our sight amid rough-hewn rocks that make our hair stand on end. The great passion of the locals for hunting chamois gave rise in the previous generation to men of great perseverance and legs of iron, who were and are

capable of following these animals right to the highest crest, shooting them and bringing their catch back on their backs. Anyone who has seen them act will come to the conclusion that they are not ordinary mortals, but legendary heroes.

The golden eagle delights us from time to time with its majestic gliding and the wallcreeper decorates the limestone with its colours. Both types of chough, the common and the alpine, will be inseparable travelling companions, and if you keep your eyes open, you may surprise a snowfinch, something of a luxury for anyone who wishes, is learning how or knows how to enjoy nature.

* = "Bastard" scree.

Above: Approaching Vega Huerta on horseback.

FROM CULIEMBRO TO THE AMUESA BYRES
III

CULIEMBRO - MONTELLUÉ - RAÍZ GULLY - TURONERO COL - CERREDO COL - AMUESA

5 km

This route does not take very long, but it is hard on the legs, although it is worth it just to have a look at the Great Wall of Amuesa, from its otherwise hidden side. Loneliness, effort, silence and clouds are our guides on this route.

Coming into Culiembro, right by the first winter byre, we can see the Cares below and a path that zigzags up the other side. A little wooden bridge, which looks tiny from where we are standing, will be our crossing point to the other bank. Opposite the house, garnished with a few walnut trees, a very steep track (the vertical difference is 350 m.) snakes its way down this way and that between screes and hawthorns. At its end is the river with clean water, fast-flowing down to the bridge. A deep and still pool serves as a mirror for the walker, and when he looks forwards, the river seems to spring uncontainable from the crag. This spot is worth a visit for its own sake, as a gorge within a gorge, of incredible beauty.

On the other side of Pando Bridge, the track climbs vertical between moistened rocks and steps that demand all our strength and our undivided attention in order not to slip. An improvised fence warns us of the possibility of ending up in the pool, but with some skill, the obstacle is overcome without any trouble. Now the real climb begins, up an almost vertical and seemingly endless slope; there is a vertical difference of over 300 m. with hardly any forward progress. Grass hides the track in places, which comes out again on the scree. With this panorama and almost leaning on the walls of Mt Llué, we come to some almost demolished win-

Facing page: The imposing Great Wall of Amuesa.

ter byres where there are goats walking about. The nettles reach an incredible height, and we must be careful not to get stung. There is a lot of mint here, though, and the shepherds say that if you are stung, you can obtain relief by rubbing the spot with the aromatic leaves of this plant.

After these winter byres, a slope of pasture comes into sight full of flowers, although the land insists on staying vertical. To sit down and rest means to be colonized by the ticks abounding all over the place here. Reaching the top and cursing our last cigarettes, we are at the Pando Gap, which offers us a side view of the Great Wall, the queen of limestone, with infinite spire-like peaks and sharp crests.

The track goes round over alpine pastures and limestone to the Raíz Gully, to go up again to the Turunero Col. Sunny days give us an unforgettable view, but when the sky is darkened by clouds, or fog creeps up the gullies, nearly everybody is overcome by a feeling of abandonment and sorrow. We have to stop and recover our strength, with the Cueva Negra ("Black Cave") spring on our left.

The track gets narrower between the rocks, and after an upward stretch we go left to reach the Cerredo Col. It is possible to continue straight ahead up the Piedra Bellida Gully to the gap itself. Either of the two tracks goes between incredible rocks, overflown only by the griffon vulture and the odd raven. The wallcreeper and the snowfinch may be seen between the crags, and there are hardly any other signs of life.

From the gap, we have the whole magnitude of the Wall at arm's length, with the River Cares on the other side. After curving round for a few metres, the track forks. To the right it goes up to the Trave slope while

ahead it goes down to the Amuesa refuge, near to the winter byre area, where the byres are open to the sky and those adventurous enough to sleep under the stars or weather a storm may spend the night. This option, told by a hillwalker, is more a chilling tale than a personal experience. Nevertheless, the invitation stands.

In the lowest part of the refuge area, a small pond sometimes forms. Here, among mountains, we enjoy some horizontal pastures, which we had almost forgotten, while with our cameras we chase a few chamois, butterflies, beetles or tiny flowers.

The adventurer feels more than rewarded for the effort of his climb. The return to the Cares path is very quick, as the erstwhile uphill slopes are now swift descents, where the legs do piecework.

The possibility exists of going to Bulnes via the Amuesa Gully, which means a descent from 1,500 m. (the refuge) to the 650 m. of the town, which can be done in three or four hours.

Above: The summit of Torre Cerredo from the Jou Negro.

TO LAKE LA ERCINA VIA THE CULIEMBRO GULLY
IV

CULLIEMBRO - OSTÓN BYRES - VEGA DE LOS CORROS ("MEADOW OF RINGS") -
VEGA MAIOR - ARNAEDO BYRES - LA GÜELGA VALLEY - BELBÍN BYRES -
BUFERRERA - LAKE LA ERCINA

10 km

At the foot of the Culiembro byre area, a track leads off with a visible upward-leading part, which goes straight to the gully of the same name. It looks foreboding from below, but once you are up, the view makes you forget the effort. The track gains height quickly, and, as usual, zigzags to make the climb easier (in a manner of speaking). Your feet notice the loose stones, but the eagerness to get up there easily overcomes these troublesome details. Taking things calmly, one can do the route in a little more than an hour and a half, although there are watering places, where we can refresh ourselves or fill our bottles. Posadorio mentions a cave near here which is large and comfortable, where the livestock is taken when the weather requires it. Again we are walking along limestone corridors, overlooking the Cares and the Great Wall of Amuesa. From here, walkers using the normal path look like ants wandering hither and thither, except for the colour of their clothes and the speed of their step.

We have a new climb up a narrow limestone gully with lichens adhering to the rock and houseleeks growing out of the cracks. Then the crag becomes meadow and the variety increases, as does the livestock. We are at the Ostón winter byres, also known popularly as the Cares observation area, as it looks out over the valley with views of heights and bottom alike. Sunny days are a blessing for the eyes, and it's a good idea to enjoy the scenery.

Facing page: In the cracks in the rock we see the very beautiful *Aquilegia discolor.*

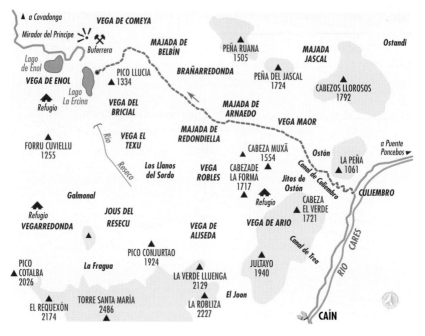

If we take the left-hand track, we'll be heading for the Montico Gully, which, not being too steep, will soon lead us to the Ario Meadow. The right-hand track, our reason for being here, takes us slowly up the La Texa Valley to the source of the Raya, which forms a small lake, in the Vega de Corros ("Meadow of Rings"). We are about 1,200 m. up and we soon come to Vega Maior ("Greater Meadow"), which takes its name from its area, which is indeed large, with groups of byres and huts built in the local style, with thick stone walls and narrow windows. As is almost to be expected, a fountain supplies the water necessary for the wayfarer and serves as a watering hole for livestock. The heights have become gentler, and the rugged terrain seems tamer, easier to walk over. A little to the left is the so-called Pozo pothole, which is not actually very deep, and which is suitable for those investigating such features for the first time.

Ahead of us is Mt Mortayales, and the track goes along next to it to the left to take us up (the climb and the distance are both short) to the Sierra Buena Gap. We are now getting near the lakes, and although we still cannot see them, the calm and peaceful scenery lets us progress at good

Facing page: The peculiar design of the Belbín byres.

speed. After the gap, we come to the Arnaedo byres, where we find a couple of shepherds having lunch. Apparently their *chorizo*[*] is made of boar meat, confirmation coming from its strong but pleasant flavour. A chinwag, a few swigs of wine and a cigarette are enough to listen to a few stories about wolves, how they attack livestock, the organization of hunting parties or Uncle Juan's feat of killing a wild boar with a pocket knife (a Taramundi one, naturally) when the snow was thick enough to slow the animal down. Besides that, the information about the route is accurate and they always give you some tip about it.

From Arnaedo, there is a gentle descent over the pasture land of the La Güelga Valley, which, with its spring, lends amplitude to this Asturian landscape given over to livestock breeding. This is where the River Castaño rises, soon to increase its flow-rate with the many tributary streams that join it, making the area enormously fertile. The downward climb is still gentle, the ground is kind on the feet and the weather calm, so the eyes wander from one side to the other meeting with byres, flowers, birds and mountains, many mountains, one after the other in endless succession.

The next byres to receive us are at Belbín. The huts are impeccable, like all the ones in the Covadonga Mountains National Park, giving a sensation of love of the land, of living according to tradition, of belonging in that environment. We cannot say the same of certain other byres, which are in an appalling state of neglect, making one wonder why they are not rebuilt to serve as shelters for hillwalkers.

A slight climb takes us up to the La Teja (or La Texa) spring, where we start the walk down to the lake, which is now in sight. Its dark blue colour contrasts with the green of the fields, the grey of the mountains and the multicoloured look of the visitors.

A gentle walk takes us down to the houses of Buferrera and the lake shore. The day has not been long and the walk has not been tiresome, though we have learnt a lot about the Picos. For this reason, it is a route that is all but compulsory for scenery lovers, with sudden and gradual changes of landscape, always full of pleasant surprises.

---

* *Chorizo*: spicy (usually pork) sausage —*translator's note.*

Facing page, top: The harsh stare of the wolf, Iberia's last superpredator.
Bottom: The beautiful apollo butterfly.

DOWN FROM THE LAKES VIA THE TREA GULLY
V

LAKE LA ERCINA - VEGA ROBLES - EL JITU - ARIO MEADOW - LAS CRUCES COL -
TREA GULLY - CUARROBLE CAVE - CARES GORGE

10 km

This is the best known route from the Lakes to the Cares Path. When done this way round, it is quite an easy route, apart from the descent of the Trea Gully. The other way round, it is so spectacular and different, that it doesn't seem the same walk, although we should have to add an hour or two to the time because of the frequent stops made to admire the scenery, delight in the tiny details it has to offer and to rest our bodies. We leave Lake La Ercina causing some consternation among the tourists around us, as we look more like a fashion parade than a group of hillwalkers, with some wearing stout boots and carrying high rucksacks, others in safari gear, and the rest...

Facing page, top: Lake Enol • *Bottom:* Lake La Ercina.

This is the shortest route between the two places, starting at the lake car park and walking round the shore to the left until we come to a path (impossible to miss) which goes past the huts leaning against Peña Lucía (1,334 m.). The climb is gentle over the lakeside meadows and after a slight slope we begin the slow descent to the Bobias byres. We are on undulating terrain used for livestock, where calves sleep in the sun or play under the watchful eye of plump, clean and peaceful cows. The heath is in flower and the spring air pervades everything. We find the first spring, next to the huts, which are well maintained, like all the ones round here, and some of them do not appear to be used for animals, judging from some of the gadgets (ice boxes, deck chairs, etc.) left outside in a combination of unreal colours. There are a couple of fine lasses sunbathing, their bodies spread with shiny creams, while the wheatear flies from rock to rock and the call of the chough reaches us from above. We frequently admire the gliding of the griffon vulture and hear the song of the cuckoo.

Above and facing page: The Picos area has in store for us one of Europe's richest floræ.

By the way, if at any time the track should disappear from your sight, then look for the cairns or little piles of stones that the shepherds and hillwalkers put there to find their way, remembering that you can always help out by building your own. Another possibility is to follow the single or double yellow marks, often faded, painted on some of the rocks.

There are two tracks ahead of us and we take the right-hand fork towards the beeches ahead, which contrast beautifully with the rocks they stand on. We make another detour as it is advisable to go up and round the trees, which makes for a gentle climb which takes us to the Llaguiello, a small pond that sometimes dries out in summer. It is in a little valley of contrasting colour, grass below and rock above. The Spanish wall lizard frequently comes out and the striking apollo butterfly flutters over the heath and gorse. With a bit of luck and attention we may catch sight of the unmistakable silhouette of the peregrine falcon perched on a crag and looking attentively over the valley, or diving in its breathtaking fashion. Where the heath is denser and the grass is thicker we may see the partridge and, of course, the highest twig is a bunting's perch.

We go up over an almost lunar landscape, made up of disperse corries

Above: Ario meadow.

(*jous*), leaving the Robles Meadow behind to take a narrow but safe and sure gully up to a noticeable point, El Jitu, which offers impressive views, as Torre Cerredo, Mt Cabrones and many other peaks appear to be within reach of one's hand, their shapes playing with the light and astonishing the hillwalker. It may be one of the most outstanding views in the Picos, though we all have our favourites. A rest is necessary, and a map table teaches us the names of many more peaks. Below us, the Ario refuge, or Marquis of Villaviciosa's refuge, set in a meadow of grass and rock, almost hanging in the gully we are about to have to go down.

The longest stretch is over, but the moment of truth is upon us. We shall begin our walk again distracted by the saxifrages growing in the rock itself, the marram grass, the woolly clary and the yellow wood violet. The track crosses the pastures at Ario, and livestock is abundant near the winter byres. The downward climb is gentle, always towards the right, until

we come to the Las Cruces Col, once atop which we are suddenly faced with the Trea Gully, over 1,100 metres of dizzy descent amid crags, hair-raising zigzags, screes, precipices and abysses, smooth faces and a thousand other quirks of nature, but it's worth it. The crag martin and the kestrel observe us from the air, the choughs seem astonished, and an Egyptian vulture flies right by us. A few beeches grow in the most incredible places, and mosses and lichens take advantage of the damp.

We soon come to Cuarroble, a cave at the top of a scree, and then, down again, even more steeply, following the marked track, our legs taking a beating while we almost feel like jettisoning the rucksack to get down more easily, but our eyes cannot avoid taking in the scenery and so we eventually come to the end of the track, twenty metres from the Bolín bridge. Making contact with the horizontal seems like a dream, and a necessary rest allows us to enjoy the delights of the Cares gorge itself "in another way".

FROM CORDIÑANES TO THE JERMOSO COL
VI

CORDIÑANES - ASOTÍN GULLY - HONDA GULLY -
SOLANO COL- TRAVIESAS DE CONGOSTO - JERMOSO COL

4 km

A classic route if ever there was one, but a hard one for the hillwalker, so it can only be recommended for those in good physical shape and with tireless legs. Those who manage to carry out such a feat, however, talk for days on end about the beauty of the crags, the worries they've been through and the effort spent, considering themselves superior beings, who have beaten the Picos de Europa. It's all very well to boast of such a prowess, but the Picos let people beat them only when they feel thus inclined, so strict care is a rule of life in these mountains. In case of doubt or hesitation, it is more sensible to turn round and enjoy an easier, though no less beautiful walk. This will never be taken as a defeat.

The route begins in Cordiñanes itself, and the track has a very obvious

Facing page: Liordes Meadow.

beginning, going gently up the Rienda Path towards the Peña del Porra-
cho, a limestone wall which is a foretaste of the route ahead. Only a few
beeches, oaks, ashes and limes break up the aspect of the rocky vastnes-
ses. Before hitting the crag, we turn left, following the rocky steps of a
hard but short climb. Once round the crag we turn back to the right to

Above: The Riendas Path to the Asotín Gully.

continue climbing, now somewhat more gently (just a manner of speaking) and taking time to get our breath back.

We soon come to a beautifully preserved beech wood, replete with life, with service trees and maples, where the tracks of weasels and beech martens abound among the holly, while Madonna lilies and bilberries together with bracken and hart's tongue carpet the ground. Roe deer are said to be plentiful, but we don't see any, and the fox comes and goes as it pleases. Goldcrests, blue tits, Bonelli's warblers, chaffinches, wrynecks, woodpeckers and great tits attract our attention, but we don't scorn the chance of a photo of a common frog or a common toad.

We continue up a reddish path, the Asotín Gully, to turn left up the Honda Gully, a tough climb over stony ground which invites us to rest every four steps. We reach the Solano Col, and Torre Jermosa, now quite near, looks like a mirage as we take in the patterns eroded into the rock, the dips where plants grow, the open spaces and the snow on the summits.

We keep on up, as always boxed in between the enormous rock masses, slipping on the thin grass and tripping over the stones, but admiring a rugged, wild, lonely and silent landscape, where the air is so thin that there isn't enough to breathe. We soon reach the Traviesas de Congosto, walking round the slope to get to the Congosto scree, where the water lets the moss grow. Chamois are frequently sighted, the golden eagle is also seen, though less often, and the wallcreeper seems to be stuck to the rock. Another tough climb up the stream takes us to a waterfall. We cross the stream and some of us go to the fountain to refresh ourselves while others, obviously with less strength left, collapse on the bank of the stream.

We are surrounded by mountains, Torre Jermosa to the left, Torre Peñalba straight ahead, Torre Llambrión to the right and others which appear and disappear with each step, the sun reflected by the white rock dazzling us, with pastureland thick with little valleys and gaps, with signs of grass in the screes, and the infinite variety of shapes of the pinnacles.

Below us, very near, is the Diego Mella refuge, small, sheltered from the wind and showing its twin chimneys as a symbol of rest. We have arrived, and all the weariness of the walk soon fades before the scenery we are privileged to enjoy.

After we get our strength back, we can set about walking back and join the Cabaña Verónica or get to the *Mirador del Cable* (Cable Observation Area) at Fuente Dé after crossing the Liordes Meadow. Both routes are very difficult walks, but after a night in the shelter talking about the day and relaxing the body, one or two are bound to be tempted to take one on.

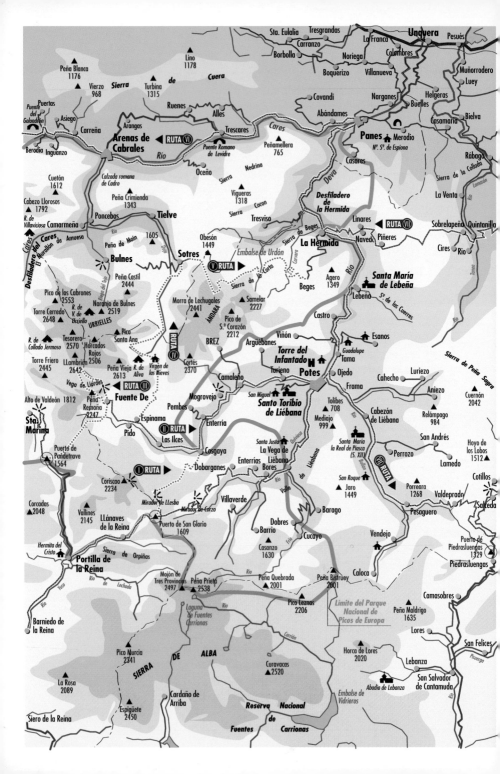

THE DEVA VALLEY

Four

RIAÑO - BOCA DE HUÉRGANO - VILLAFREA DE LA REINA - ESPEJOS
DE LA REINA - BARNIEDO DE LA REINA - PORTILLA DE LA REINA -
LLÁNAVES DE LA REINA - SAN GLORIO PASS - MIRADOR DEL CORZO ("ROE DEER
OBSERVATION AREA") - LA VEGA DE LIÉBANA ("LIÉBANA MEADOW") - POTES

56 km

This route takes us from the Leonese side to Potes, something of a nerve centre for many other outings. Though it doesn't look like it, we have at our disposal three possibilities, or different walks, each with its own special features, and all of them certainly meeting the strictest demands. The first one is the made-up road down the San Glorio Pass, the second is from the Pandetrave Pass, which has the advantage of leading us direct to Fuente Dé, where we'll be sheltered by Peña Remoña; while the third one is via the Senda del Oso ("Bear Path"), a name not used by the locals (who have many different names for it), but bestowed by hillwalkers on a path which will obviously leave a great impression on you, while at the same time paying homage to that almost extinct and mythical animal, a meeting with which in the middle of the forest is desired by all Nature lovers, and whose preservation directly affects our code of ethics.

We shall describe the route beginning at the Riaño end. As a precautionary measure before starting out, it is necessary to find out the state of any snow on the pass, as it is easily closed and snowfalls are quite common round here, not being at all rare in spring and autumn.

Just after leaving Riaño, we take the N-621 road towards the pass, seeing the mountains reflected in the water of the reservoir, which later on, about mid morning, will be criss-crossed by the wakes of the motorboats that are gradually colonizing the jetty. Hardly have we started out when we go over a viaduct, leaving to our left an intact virgin beech wood, the Ormas Forest, a refuge for the bear, the capercaillie and for many other species of plants and animals, a protected area in which we shall on no account set foot if indeed we wish to preserve species in serious danger of extinction.

We go down a gentle slope into the valley and reach Boca de Huérgano, linked to tradition by its stone houses yet in a present aimed at tourism, with abundant hostelries. We must look down from the Roman bridge, with three arches, into a River Yuso replete with trout and with its banks lined with trees, where the willows don't let us see some of the birds, representative of which is the dipper, which is accompanied in its dives by the Pyrenean desman. On leaving, we are received by wide, horizontal and well watered fields, where the daffodils manage to drown the green of the grass with their yellow every spring, year after year without fail, although they may sometimes be a few days late if the weather is not good, which, by the way, is quite likely. A long straight stretch takes us to Villafrea de la Reina, on the right, with the lower slopes covered in heath and broom, beech trees at the top and oak in between, with a mixture of birch, service trees and holly. We are now in an area of red deer, whose figures may be admired at dawn and dusk after patient observation (and with a good pair of binoculars). A few crows and ravens fly over the valley. Almost at once we come to Los Espejos de la Reina, beside a River Yuso with a healthy flow-rate, clean water and a well-preserved gallery forest, with Barniedo just off the route.

A few bends announce the pass that awaits us, and the valley gets narrower, the mountains get higher, and the river is right next to us. We come to a junction, going past Portilla de la Reina on our right and carry straight on to a first ravine, where the moss-covered puddingstone makes the road bend while the river makes its way in a series of jumps past enormous rocks that attempt in vain to thwart its path. Every crack seeps with water and a few vultures are to be seen when we look up.

Suddenly we see the first houses of Llánaves de la Reina, a small compact village offering rest to the traveller, combining new and old and maintaining a style between the two. It's a good place to start walking tours in the mountains, the first hours after dawn being the best, when the roe deer are grazing in the valleys and the red deer are walking around halfway up the slopes. The road, by the way, is narrow and the beginning of the pass is already upon us. The beginning is gentle, with fine views of fields with daffodils and mountainsides covered in heather and crags, where red deer abound and the autumn rutt (after the first rain) is quite a show. We should never forget to chat with the forestry wardens, as we won't only learn the best possibilities but we'll avoid putting our foot in it when it comes to the special laws governing these areas.

The successive bends of the recently made-up road don't stop till we get to the top of San Glorio, on the provincial boundary and a natural place to look over the three provinces, an endless space for a view over the Cereceda Valley, with Mt Rabadorio (2,056 m.) on the right, its slopes populated with beech trees and where life is abundant in the shape of an attractive floral cover and a varied fauna. To the left, on clear days, you can see the summits of the Central and Western Massifs, and when the fog hangs low, the sea of cloud makes you think you're in Heaven itself. The only discordant sight is the pines planted on terraces to your right, forming an evergreen mass that doesn't belong with the real scenery of this environment.

The downward slope is steep - well, rather than steep, staggering, with hairpin bends that disorientate us and upset the stomachs of some of the occupants of the car, till we get to the (popularly called) Roe Deer observation area, after the animal statue dominating the valley, the beech woods, the pastures, the Peñas de la Horcada (1,770 m.), Peña Bricia (1,281 m) and hundreds of ridges in symmetrical succession. With calm and binoculars we can see roe deer, chamois, buzzards and kestrels, and

Following double page: San Glorio, Peña Prieta Massif *(top left)*. Villafrea *(bottom left)*. From the Llesba Col *(top right)*. Autumn in Llánaves *(bottom right)*.

when the light fades, the snipe flies overhead and the barn owl and the little owl start their song.

We continue down in a dive, round more bends, past Enterrías and Bores and, on the right, is the turn-off for Dobres and Cucayo, at the feet of Pico Palanca (1,662 m.) and near Peña Bistuey (2,001 m.), a recommendable outing for the enjoyment of Cantabrian mountain scenery. From Cucayo, you can get to the small but charming village of Puente de Ranes, and, following the stream to the right, to the winter byres of Escobal de Tejedo and Prado de Toro, thence to gain the very base of Peña Prieta (2,536 m.), where a small lake will reflect the tiredness on your faces. It should always be born in mind that the less known routes may be the most beautiful, as hillwalking also is subject to fashion.

The descent becomes gentler and, past La Vega, the scenery changes, with meadows and large traditional houses, a mild climate and an all-pervasive vegetation. The river supports a dense

Above: Vada and the River Quiviesa • *Facing page:* Enterrías.

fringing forest and there is a very varied birdlife. We cross the River Quiviesa to enter the lower part, where grazing land and livestock dominate the landscape and the activity of the locals is clearly that way inclined, though the services for tourists are not to be sneezed at. Straight stretches are more common and the temperature rises quickly, favouring the growth of vegetation, with admirable ashes and alders giving way to the occasional beech. The fauna responds to the climate, and the robin, night-ingale, wren and blackcap are abundant, and the blackbird, great tit, song thrush and long-tailed tit are also to be seen. Further on to the right there remains a stand of cork oaks (not visible from the road), which makes a wonderful walk to keep enjoying the fauna, where the whinchat and the chaffinch con-template the activities of buzzards, ravens, honey buzzards and, with luck, the peregrine falcon. For the lover of animals living nearer the ground there is the ocellated lizard, the Spanish wall

Following double page: Monastery of St Toribio of Liébana *(left).* Mogrovejo *(top).* Reclining effigy of St Toribio *(middle).* St Toribio of Liébana *(bottom).*

133

lizard, the common wall lizard and an endless variety of insects colonizing the heather, rock roses, thyme, arbutus, oaks and holm oaks, making extremely beautiful subjects for photography.

Moments later we come to Potes, a charming town of tourists and farmers, where the taste of tradition is not lost with the passage of time and whose character has not been changed by the enormous number of visitors. The centre is the old part, whose narrow streets are an ideal place to loose oneself in, be it by day or by night. It has life, bustle and shops, with bars serving *tapas*, restaurants with local valley food and discothèques for those who like staying up late, all depending on one's plans for the following day and the heaviness of the sheets. There is a great deal to do here, and it is certainly worth while to be guided round crags and valleys by professionals.

Above: Iberian rock lizard, an interesting and harmless reptile.
Preceding double page: Potes, the Infantado Tower (Town Hall).

THE SENDA DEL OSO ("BEAR PATH")

I

SAN GLORIO - LLESBA COL - MIRADOR DEL OSO ("BEAR OBSERVATION AREA") - LA
GUARDA COL - COJORCOS WINTER BYRES - COSGAYA

19 km

We already know the way to San Glorio from the previous route. Right at the top, a path leads off to the left which takes us to the monument to the bear. Any car can get to the base, as long as the path hasn't been muddied by rain. Be careful not to skid, easy to do in such conditions and with unpleasant consequences.

The climb to the monument is 150 m. up a sloping field, but the view is well worth the effort, the panorama is almost never-ending and the typical photo is a great souvenir. For the most insatiable, the climb to the

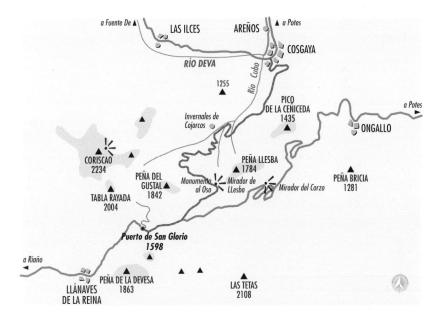

crags on the left will afford an even greater view, and, what's more, the possibility of showing off before those who have sat down at the bear's feet. If we follow the path, we'll come to the Guarda Gap, where a few crags will serve as a look-out post to give us an idea of the route we're going to take. Below us is Cosgaya, its red roofs showing up against the green fields. In between is a well-preserved beech wood, which we must go through, with, in the distance, the cirque of mountains of Fuente Dé, with such major peaks as Peña Remoña (2,227 m.), Peña Olvidada ("The Forgotten Crag") (2,406 m.), Peña Vieja ("The Old Crag") (2,627 m.), which block our view of Mt Naranjo (2,519 m.), but whose presence we sense behind the snows, almost as a lure to make us keep following the route. For those who do the route the other way round, it should be said that motorists will have no problems, but cyclists will have to work very hard to get up the steep slopes, quite a few having to pick their machines up and carry them.

Heath and broom take up the higher parts of the slopes, and the mountain pastures look like irregularly patterned green carpets with the shapes of opulent cows moving over them. Butterflies and flowers abound, while moles make their hills of loose fertile earth as they excavate their tunnels. We cross a field to begin the steep downward climb, coming across the first trees, birches, whose silver bark gives an accurate indication of the upper limit of woodland. Then come the beeches, stunted at first, but then higher-boled as we go down. A large shed serves as a winter byre for livestock. The bends are very sharp and really put the driver's skill to the test, a three-point turn being necessary on one of them. Water seeps out everywhere, giving rise to small brooks that will gradually join together to form the River Cubo, a leaping stream as is obligatory for a mountain river, with pools and torrents working the course and permitting the presence of the Pyrenean desman, not at all easy to find, but quite a visual kick when seen moving around under the water.

On the left-hand slope there is heath and broom, juniper and hawthorn, and limestone, always limestone, as small stones, large boulders or impressive crags, just asking to be climbed. Disperse rowan and whitebeam appear, in season their red fruit contrasting beautifully with the green background. Hazels grow like candles, unbending, and a few willows and alders grow near the water. Down next to the ground, dense clumps of bracken grow in the shade, and mosses and lichens carpet trunks and rocks, while wild strawberry and bilberry offer their fruit res-

---

Facing page, top: From the Bear Observation Area • *Middle:* Harebell • *Bottom:* Grazing land at the Llesba Col.

pectively in summer and autumn. As usual, the jay kicks up a racket as it flies in front of the car, frightening the roe deer but without taking away our hope of sighting a capercaillie, the emblem of the beech wood, synonym of freedom and purity, and unseeing lover in spring.

At a bend the track forks; in front of us, across the river, are the Cojorcos winter byres and, continuing downwards, is our path. Here to stop is a must, it is a beautiful spot to take a few photos and chase some toad that doesn't want to pose in front of the camera. From here on the river leaps over waterfalls and its beaten waters splash the banks where bracken grows thick, and bird song may come from anywhere. From the clearings in the beech wood it is possible to see the other side, covered in heath and young oaks, while the path becomes easier to follow. The fox sleeps stretched out in the sun against a background of crags, as if curious about what's going on in the village.

The scenery changes, opening up towards the valley floor, and a herd of goats blocks our path. Soon a goatherd arrives on a moped to gather the animals, and leads us at a wearying pace to the beginning of the vil-

Above and facing: Two beautiful parts of the Bear Path.

lage. Almost at the entrance to the village we see a few holm oaks, synonymous with a milder climate, with limes, cherry trees, service trees and alders, through which there appear small fields, some with wooden fences, others divided by hedgerows, where birds find excellent look-out posts. The village of Cosgaya is not particularly small, and its houses are spread out over the mountainsides, so much so that some of them seem to be hanging from the fields. Small gardens supply the larders of the houses, both renovated and old, in a combination of tradition and summer tourism.

The cement streets take us to a steep slope that goes down to a huge monolithic rock, standing like an unmoving stone look-out in our way. Two hundred metres further on we join the asphalt road, by a modern bridge built to look like a Roman one, covered in ivy, which contrasts with the grey of the stone. To the right, 14 km. away, is Potes, and 5.5 km. to the left is Espinama. Ahead of us is the River Deva, a salmon stream, bordered by a thick beech wood, holm oaks that seem to climb the rocks, and well-kept fields. The road surface is impeccable, and the chain of fields, fences, beech trees, willows, alders and a great number of hostelries are our travelling companions to Potes.

FROM SANTA MARINA TO POTES VIA PEDAVEJO
II

SANTA MARINA - PEÑAS DE CIFUENTES - PEDAVEJO GULLY - LAS BERRUGAS WIN-
TER BYRES - FUENTE DÉ - ESPINAMA - LAS ILCES - COSGAYA - AREÑOS - TREVIÑO
- ENTERRÍA - BESOY - BARCENA - CAMALEÑO - BARÓ - TURIENO - POTES

42 km

We set out from Santa Marina for Pandetrave along an asphalt path which is extremely narrow, but free of danger, amid very rich pastures, majestic trees and modern buildings abandoning the traditional style. Very soon the road widens and we climb up towards the pass, commanding an ever-improving view of a valley that recedes into the distance and whose villages shrink away before our eyes. Heights and distances can be incredible in the Picos, where everything is far away and near at the same time.

Facing page: Santa Marina, with Torre Bermeja in the background.
Following double page: Peña Remoña *(top left).* Torre Friero and Torre Salinas *(bottom left).* Pido *(top right).* Espinama *(bottom right).*

145

At the top, a track goes off to the left (it isn't signposted, but it's the only one), with a good surface and quite even, surrounded by heather and livestock, which soon lets us see the border of birches, then the beech wood, and, below us, the fields of Los Llanos, Valdeón, to then turn towards the Cifuentes Valley.

We soon come to a junction; to the left we can go to the Heights of Valdeón (1,834 m.), to reach the Pedabejo Spring, sheltered by the Peñas de Cifuentes, with the Torre de Salinas (2,446 m.) a step away if we are willing to climb up slippery screes or cross by the Pedabejo Gully, a longer trip, but a much safer one.

The right-hand fork takes us around the limestone on one side, with heath- and broom-covered ridges on the other. We begin the descent into a wide valley well supplied with livestock in its fields, while dwarf juniper covers much of the stony ground. Five km from the beginning of the path we come to a gate to keep the animals in, that just lets the car through, at the beginning of a well-preserved birchwood, where the white trunks stand out against the colouring of the background. The beeches get progressively taller as we drive further down, and there are many service trees and holly bushes. The wayside is colonized by brambles, and the fields abound in asphodel. A jay flies across with its beak full of food and Amelia insists on following it to get the photo of the year, with the chicks in the hypothetical nest. An hour's wait and the look of frustration on the photographer's face make us waive any comment and we set off down again in sepulchral silence.

The track crosses to the other side, leaving the company of the wood to advance amid broom, heath with its white flowers and yellow-flowered gorse, a veritable design in colouring which certainly makes up for the bumpy ride. The vales boast roe deer at dawn, while the lord of the heather is the red deer.

Soon another beech copse shades the track, now near the crag, where steep sloping pastures don't stop the cows grazing. Every so often a little brook springs forth from just anywhere, to end up as part of the river Cantiján, which in turn offers up its waters to the Deva. Willows, somewhat stunted, afford shade to the transparent waters, while a legion of butterflies adds colour to the scene.

Shortly afterwards, we come to a cement trough, with a pipe that continuously supplies it with cool water, though more water is lost over one

Facing page, top: Towards the Pandetrave byres • *Bottom:* Traditional *hórreos* at Santa Marina de Valdeón.
Following double page: The Western Massif from Pandetrave.

of its sides than comes in. It is the Valjierro Fountain, from which to the right we can see the Quebres beechwood colonizing the slopes; to the left is bare limestone and ahead is the valley, where beech-covered ridges fade into the distance by the hundred, giving the view a sensation of infinity. Pido and Espinama appear on the valley floor, with fields of varying sizes, very green, amid a thick vegetation vibrant with the unceasing song of hundreds of birds. We are in sight of Peña Remoña (2,227 m.), accessible from this side by crossing the Bregón Gully, the last part of which is frankly very steep, although the view it commands makes the adventure of the walk up worthwhile. In the distance is Peña Vieja (The Old Crag, 2,612 m.), still with snow on its summit, serving as a reminder of the tremendous heights reached by these pointed limestone masses.

We soon come to a junction where the road to the right almost sends us back the way we came. We carry on straight ahead, finding wrens, blackcaps and green woodpeckers. The rock forms agglomerates with vegetation growing in every crack, the screes hardly bear any yellow lichen, while further down, juniper, Spanish broom, heather and broom of different sizes abound. Small lateral valleys point their fields into the beech wood, conferring a great visual wealth on the scenery, with the promise of getting a good view of the roe deer, so common in the area. Some ridges are all but completely covered with clumps of gorse, their yellow flowers looking like half-heartedly arranged pot plants. We return to the beechwood, with the rush of the river sounding below us, the white hawthorn blossom and the hues of the rowan with its velvety leaves standing out together with the noisy flight of the woodpigeon, which almost blankets out the sound of any other bird.

Again we come to a gate, and another trough, the one at the La Jaya Fountain, at the top of a steep descent that will take us down through a mixed beechwood into the valley. A few oaks prosper among the beeches, the ground being covered with a fine short and thick grass. After a bend, the three winter byres at Las Berrugas tell us of a thriving livestock-breeding activity, while we see more and more hazels and fewer and fewer beech trees. Now we can see the whole corrie of Fuente Dé, hundreds of limestone peaks vying with each other to be the highest, cut almost vertically and astonishing the traveller with so many different shapes, so many different shades of grey, that time goes by without us noticing it and we take an unending series of photos.

Another trough, provided with a very generous pipe, gives birth to a

Preceding double page: The Fuente Dé Corrie.

stream permitting the growth of bracken and moss all around. After the winter byre, the track gets gentler as it goes past the camp site and reaches the made-up road, a few metres from the cableway and the Fuente Dé *parador nacional**.

We are 22 km. from Potes, and the road is downhill with an impeccable surface, allowing us to enjoy the scenery of the valley floor, where livestock breeding and tourism function side by side, although the latter seems to have the upper hand. We pass Espinama, its elongated fields divided by straight wires ending at the Deva riverside, with its thick fringing forest; Los Ilces with its welcome for tourists, and Besoy, Camaleño and Baró, with inns and hotels, new houses that blend in with the surroundings, hardly distinguishable from the old ones, and the holm oaks, the sign of a temperate climate, with mild winters allowing outings at any time, to reach Potes, with its ever-crowded streets.

* State-owned hotel. Most are three-star - *translator's note*.

Above: The Fuente Dé Fall.

TO THE LIORDES MEADOW
III

FUENTE DÉ - CABLE OBSERVATION AREA - LA COLLADINA -
HOYOS DE LLOROZA - COLLADINA DE LAS NIEVES -
HOYOS DE LOS LAGOS - LAKE BAJERO - LIORDES MEADOW -
LIORDES TORNOS - EMBUDO ("FUNNEL") GULLY - FUENTE DÉ

10 km

The route is designed to provide two different kinds of enjoyment at the same time: the journey up in the cable car and the onslaught of rock against boot as we take in the scenery.

The cable car is safe and lets you drink in a spectacular landscape as it goes swiftly up, almost vertically over the last stretch, where you get a real bird's eye view, and distances and slopes seem to take on new measurements. This way of flying with your feet on the floor leaves your hands

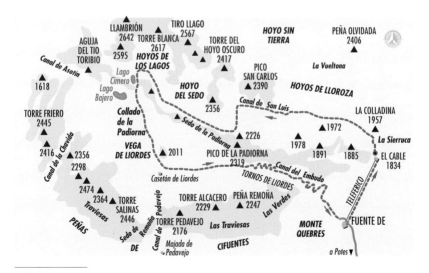

Facing page: A privileged perspective of the Cable Observation Area *(top)*. Cableway *(bottom)*.

free to shoot away with your camera and let your imagination wander like a golden eagle's.

Once back on terra firma, at the Cable observation area (1,834 m.), we can look out over the fields of Buseco, the extensive beechwoods covering the slopes, and the limestone mass, huge, unstoppable with a thousand different shapes and arêtes, making up a world of stone where only snow seems to belong. We are in the subalpine zone, with small meadows of short grass, much favoured by chamois, and a few Spanish gorse bushes, of stunted growth to withstand the wind that always blows in these parts.

Choughs, both common and alpine, openly allow their photographs to be taken, as if wishing us luck on our journey, which we shall begin by taking the track with Mt La Colladina (1,927 m.) on its right. A few vultures glide above, their relaxed flight in direct contrast with the activity of the snowfinch. If we are watchful, we may see a wallcreeper, a beautiful bird with a slender curved bill and red and white plumage that decorates the rock as it flutters. Shortly afterwards, a sharp bend to the right indicates the path leading off to the left, which is the one we must take, around the Hoyos de Lloroza, where we can see a little lake or pool and spiny gorse bushes.

The path begins to lead up into the San Luis Gully, and to the right we have the Torre de Altaiz (2,335 m.) and the Pico San Carlos (2,390 m.). Had we taken the 4WD track, we would now be on the other side of these peaks, over by the old mines of Altaiz.

The last stretch of the gully is a steep but short climb ending with a view of the Hoyo Oscuro, with its horseshoe-shaped limestone corrie blocking our way. We turn left towards the Colladina de las Nieves, at the feet of the Pico la Padiorna (2,319 m.), where submerged in the rock which is now all around us, we find Spanish gorse, dwarf juniper and bearberry, with an endless succession of peaks, gaps and gullies, and have to consult the map continually to sort out the different colossi surrounding us. Patches of snow still lie in the shadows, while in the sun the common wall lizard rests, impervious to the caws of the ravens, but fast in its flight when a photographer comes near.

A rest is a must, and our binoculars help us find a few groups of chamois, some far away, others much nearer, which, with patience, luck and a good telephoto lens, allow us to take a few photos. Herds of chamois

Preceding double page: Lloroza Corries *(left)*. Lloroza Wells *(top)*. Chamois on a snow patch on Mt Lloroza *(middle)*. Peña Remoña *(bottom)*.

move about slowly, frequently resting. There are a few young ones that do not move far away from their mothers, while the rest graze on the sparse grass of these heights. Again, patient observation will help us find the odd fox, which will no doubt be awaiting the right moment to capture a kid.

Back on the move, we have to cross some rocky areas, where it is difficult to keep one's balance and it's easy to slip up. A few ferns grow close to the sparse soil, and a few flowers, like toadflax and dandelion lend a little colour to the rock, from which the vegetation hangs in an unlikely balance. Now the path is comfortable, almost flat, until we come to a place where we can see Lake Cimero, in the Hoyo de los Lagos. To our left there appears a narrow gully, which we cross to find Lake Bajero and to follow the track, which now doubles back on itself, that is, leading to the Cable observation area. The Iberian rock lizard, with its intense eye-catching green colour, consumes a good helping of photographs, at the same time as we begin the descent towards the Vega de Liordes ("Liordes Meadow"). Here part of the rock is covered by grass, and in the deepest part, the ground gets waterlogged, permitting the presence of plant species unique to the area, but in such low numbers that they are threatened with extinction. Leaving the Liordes refuge behind us we go past the old mines to begin the climb down the Liordes *tornos**.

There is a name that you will never forget, the *Canal del Embudo* (Funnel Gully), an extremely narrow passage with a certain incline, well, more of a suicidal drop in fact, hewn from the living rock, where all our attention is focused on the tips of our boots. Then the gully opens up, with Peña Remoña beside it, with a large and well-preserved beechwood at its feet, in direct contrast with the previous scenery. The path zigzags down dizzily, making the legs go weak, so that we continually stop, making use of our rests to contemplate the Fuente Dé corrie, the flight of the chough and the multicoloured bustle of tourists queuing up for the cable car, which you will get to after a walk across a few fields, your face twisted by suffering, and your legs ruined, a sure sign of impending stiffness, but with the immense satisfaction of having brought off quite a feat.

Of course this route can be done the other way round, but when you see the climb awaiting you from the base, you will surely follow the recommendation to do it the way we propose.

---

* A *torno* is a steep zigzag path cut into the mountainside by shepherds - *translator's note*.

FROM ESPINAMA TO SOTRES
IV

ESPINAMA - IGÜEDRI WINTER BYRES - LAS LLAVIAS BYRES - ÁLIVA REFUGE - LOMA DEL TORO ("BULL RIDGE") - WAYSIDE CHAPEL OF OUR LADY OF THE SNOWS - LA RAYA ("THE LINE") - SOTRES MEADOW - FRESNIDIELLO MEADOW - CABAO WINTER BYRES - SOTRES

20 km

This is surely one of the classic routes for the 4WD, a mechanical invention that allows us to cover distances that on foot would suppose a great physical effort and the availability of many hours of free time. So, we'll show a scrupulous respect for the environment and won't let the wheels of our vehicle go a single centimetre off the track. Enjoyment has to be, and is, synonymous with preservation, which in turn is only possible given a sound environmental education. We shall not cease to prove that we are worthy of the name travellers.

In Espinama, in the middle of the village, the track begins that takes us on this adventure. The surface is good, it's about as wide as a motorway and the slope isn't to be sneezed at, but the bends can be taken with no difficulty, though a few bikers whizz by like lightening, their hurry totally incomprehensible. We go up through a beechwood, where a few hazels and fewer service trees add another colour to the scenery while bringing out the dominance of the beech, which hinders the greater biodiversity of other similar areas. Fields appear on the opposite slope, reaching down to the course of the River Nervandi, a trickle in the summer but a torrent after the spring thaw. Above our heads, bare limestone can now be seen, a mere foretaste of what is going to be the dominant scenery.

Past a bend we come to the Igüedri winter byres, well kept and of fair size, some with nettles round them, showing how little they have been used in recent years. A small ravine takes the track down to the river, and

---

Facing page: From Áliva to the Cable Observation Area, with the Old Crag in the background.

163

after going through a gate for keeping livestock in, we come into an area of huge mountain meadows where livestock is plentiful and one's gaze hits hard up on bare mountains. We come to the first junction, where we turn left to come straight away to another fork. To the left, past a pool that keeps its water in thanks to its plasticized bottom and where the no bathing sign is clearly visible, we come to the Áliva refuge, amid this splendid landscape, a good place for the first rest and for refreshments, if necessary. The track continues up, past the Chalet Real ("Royal House"), to the Cable observation area itself, posing no difficulty for the 4WD, as long as the snow hasn't left any trenches we can't get round.

From the refuge, or via the right-hand fork at the previous junction, we come to a pass. If we continue ahead we'll go down to the River Duje, almost by its source, to follow a track that gradually gets worse and worse. A pool apparently emanating from the very rock muddies the ground, and tadpoles appear in their hundreds where the water is shallowest. At the end of the track are the (now disused) Mánforas mines, which gave a brown blende, before which we go over an old moraine that takes

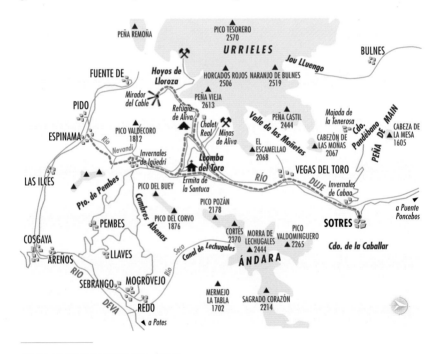

Facing pages: Toro winter byres, Sotres.

164

us to the Juan de la Cuadra Range, with Mt. Garmona (2,286 m.), the Old Crag (Peña Vieja, 2,613 m.) and the Forgotten Crag (Peña Olvidada, 2,406 m.) a mere step away. Continuing on foot via the Canal del Vicario ("Vicar's Gully"), we'll be on one of the turnings leading to the Úbeda refuge after we go down the La Celada Gully, at the very feet of Mt Naranjo of Bulnes, which is on our left.

Returning to the previous pass, the track goes down the crest itself, known as the Llomba de Toro ("Bull's Back") with a view to the right of the wayside chapel (*ermita*) of Our Lady of the Snows or of the *Santuca* of Áliva (it answers to both names), greatly revered by the local animal handlers, as, in answer to their prayers here, many of their charges have been saved from the unforeseen and abundant snowfalls that occur here. The chapel is in the most protected part of the valley, in the middle of the fields that lead up to the crags and timidly up the screes to disappear in the cracks, the grass watered by snow patches that cannot withstand the summer heat without melting. To the left we have another valley, with huge screes hanging on Mt. La Garmona (2,286 m.), Mt. Cueto de la Cuadra (2,231 m.) and the Paredón del Albo (2,125 m.), in a landscape typical of the Picos de Europa, formed by the erosive action of wind, rain and ice, which break up the rocks to form veritable rivers of stone, which are not without their mobility.

We are now in the valley of the Duje, whose course is enlarged at each step by melting snow and streams coming down from the summits. After passing, on our right, Mt El Jiso (2,178 m.), Mt Prao Cortés (2,288 m.) and Mt Cortés (2,373 m.) we come to La Raya ("The Line"), a perfectly straight line of barbed wire set on evenly spaced posts and interrupted only by the gate we have to go through, which blocks the path of livestock animals, to the greater peace of mind of their owners. The valley narrows into a ravine dominated by limestone, ever shining, ever inviting you to climb and offering adventure. Once over the river, a little unevenness of the track making the ride bumpy for the passengers of the car, some of whom demand a lower speed, we come to the meadows (Vegas) of El Toro, or Sotres, a major byre centre with over twenty buildings, most of them in good condition, a few with their tiles on the ground. It is a meeting point for many travellers, who camp here by the river, sheltered by the crags, some in tiny tents, others in what look like stately homes, depending on what system of propulsion they've used to get here (boots, bike, 4WD).

Facing page: Cabao winter byres.

The day is sunny, and swimwear contrasts with white or over-red skin, as the sun of the mountains is sneaky, and constant precautions are requi-red.

A few ups and downs in the track tax the shock absorbers, and the sce-nery around us is rocky slopes and grazing land. Soon we come to the Fresnidiello Meadow, with green fields divided by stone walls, which we see after going up a knoll to see Sotres, set halfway up the slope, surroun-ded by greenery, against which the red of its roof tiles stands out, and limited by the ever-present limestone. The Duje, which we have not left for a moment, dazzles us with its clear waters on a milkwhite bed. On both sides, there are almost as many great limestone caves as there are peaks. Goats begin to be a regular feature of the landscape, and black and blue butterflies abound in the fields and down by the river. The raven does not go unnoticed and the wheatear frequently appears. As we appro-ach the El Texu winter byres, the white wagtail becomes our inseparable travelling companion.

This page: Romería of Our Lady of Health • *Facing page:* Sotres, from La Caballar.
*See footnote on page 239.

When we reach the byres, the track forks. To the left, over the river, it zigzags up to Vega de les Cuerres, continuing as a path as far as Mt Naranjo of Bulnes, probably being the most popular route for admiring this myth from nearby. We continue ahead, down across steeply sloping fields that reach down to the beech trees that cover the limestone, always leaving the summits bare but covering the rounded tops of the foothills. We hit asphalt, and the change is spectacular, not only in the comfort of the traveller, but also in the new scenery unfolding before us, where the beech trees sieve the light, the fields are an intense, almost violent, green, and vultures glide in the sky over Sotres. The sight and the setting of the village are unrepeatable, but the houses are losing tradition, and *Uralita**, modern architecture and a construction free-for-all are causing æsthetic pollution in one of the nicest parts of the Picos de Europa. Preservation entails maintaining traditions and respecting them amid the expansion of tourism, and having strict laws to stop such outrages.

---

* *Uralita* (regd. trademark) is a synthetic material, usually green or brown, often used for roofing - *translator's note.*

FROM SOTRES TO BEGES VIA THE TEJO BEND
V

SOTRES - LA CABALLAR COL - MONTE LA ESCAMPADA - JITO DE ESCARANDI - LA
JAZUCA BYRES - SIERRA DE BEGES - TEJO BEND - HOJA COL - BEGES

18 km

Another classic route for the 4WD, but with the obvious difficulties of
a narrow track where the hairpin bends make the nose of the vehicle
disappear from the sight of the driver, who cannot help but utter a few
hastily cobbled-together prayers. However, a little prudence, a certain
amount of skill and some disregard for the car can make the route an
unforgettable delight some of us will tell our grandchildren about.

From Sotres over an asphalt road we start up a winding slope between
large and steep fields, bordered by great oak trees in clumps, and patches
of beechwood dispersed over the hillsides to create a review of scenery
types of great chromatic and picturesque beauty. A few horses give a

Facing page, top: Track from Sotres to Beges • *Bottom:* La Llama.

touch of movement to the scene as we go up to the La Caballar Col, where the winter byres are forgetting their former use to become summer resting places. From one of these shacks comes forth a raucous and excessively loud music, setting the feathers on edge of the few ravens that dare come near. Anyway, if you walk along the path that leads off to the right, you'll come to a natural observation area over the Sotres valley, with the Escampada area and the Pica de Fuente Soles (1,564 m.) to your left. Opposite is the Eastern Massif, no less, and behind us are ridges covered in heath and gorse, with the obvious marks of several fires in a contrast that makes you stop and think.

The road runs over the uncultivated ridges, past Braña Espina on the right round a wide bend that then bends the other way to come to the Jito de Escarandi, 3.6 km. from Sotres. A widened area to the right is the only sign of the track, as there is no signpost. Anyway you will see a sign written with a mauve paint spray saying "to the Ándara refuge".

The descent begins straight away, down the La Arrudo slope, with a more-than-uneven surface where the slowness of the vehicle is funda-

Above: Daffodils cover the fields, heralding spring.

172

mental. We go past Era del Torco (1,381 m.) on the left, and crags with vegetation clinging into every crack, to go down into the valley past a beautiful beechwood with trees growing between the rocks. There are a lot of flowers, and many beetles and butterflies colonize the grasses, in the viewfinders of our cameras. Soon, also on the left, the uncluttered and gently undulating fields let us see the La Jazuca byres, in a privileged nook of silence, light and scenery that turn it bucolic in a flash. A slight uphill climb takes us back to the beechwood, where the screes are winning ground from the slope, heath edges the meadows and the livestock rests with great indolence.

The track changes, not in its surface, but in its appearance, as it is now narrow, with the crags to the right and a sheer drop to the left, with hairpin bends that make it necessary for the drivers of longer 4WDs to make three-point turns. A few muffled cries of nervousness are uttered by our friends, but the landscape helps to calm the situation. We come to a sharp bend where a path goes off to the right and we walk down it to the Ándara refuge, where many people have gathered and the views are fantastic. We take the path marked by thousands of boots to the Ándara well, where the presence of two lakes changes the look of the scenery, with the Mazarrasa mines on the other side. The path carries on past the crossings of Grajal de Abajo and Grajal de Arriba, over screes and surrounded by a corrie, past Pico Valdominguero (2,265 m.), round and over the mountains to Sotres. A nice outing lasting 5 or 6 hours.

After the double bend at Ándara, we go over to the other side, onto open country that lets us enjoy a very diverse scenery, with the La Jazuca Gully below us, the winter byres set in the fields, an enormous limestone cave that seems to keep thousands of secrets with a path zigzagging up to it, daring the walker to approach, and the winter byres, disperse, perched atop the abyss in incredible parts of fields set on the very crags, with screes at every turn. It's a rugged but charming view of the Picos, with surprises round every bend, changes in every valley, every day, every moment.

Going round the mountainside (the track is still just as narrow), we come to the Macondiú Wall, with the peak of the same name, exactly 2,000 m. high, on the right. The track forks and the right-hand fork can take us to the Vegas de Ándara ("Ándara Meadows"), with another spectacular change of scenery. This stretch has very sharp bends climbing quickly up the mountainside, with stones, an uneven surface and other ingredients to satisfy the hankerings of the 4WD lover. As you go up, you

can see Mt Llama, the Sierra de Beges and the Las Brañas Pass. The fields have thinner grass, but the sheep are abundant, and we are completely surrounded by rocks. Once at Vegas de Ándara, the view more than makes up for our suffering in the car, for right opposite our eyes is a circle of arêtes and screes with Mt Junciana (2,267 m.) and the Pico del Sagrado Corazón ("Peak of the Sacred Heart"), parts of the Sierra Mojones no less awe-inspiring than any other part of the massif. The return to the Beges track has to be undertaken unhurriedly, as it now seems even narrower and the abysses even deeper (he who warns...).

We continue down to see hundreds of valleys eating back between as many mountains, with patches of beechwood sprinkled over the landscape. The buzzard is lord of the air while in front of us are only a few pipits and wheatears.

The path slopes seriously to reach the double bend of Concha Varera (1,583 m.), with the Riega de los Lobos letting its waters run down, the

This page: Zigzag ascent to Tresviso • *Facing page:* Winter byres at La Jacuza.

Sierra de Beges as the final horizon and the Corvera Canyon like a mess of different limestones drawn by a modernist artist. We then turn round towards the other valley to get to the Tejo bend, with its unrepeatable view over Mt Llama and the Sierra de la Corta, with its disperse patches of beechwood and fields straddling the cols. All that's missing is the yew, the mythical tree revered by the Celts, and whose poisonous seeds were used by Asturian warriors.

The slopes are awesome, the engine sounds hoarse and the bumpiness of the ride throws the passengers out of their seats while at the same time affording us a none-to-reassuring view of the abyss. We come to a junction. To the left we could go back to the beginning of the route by a different and no less complicated way. We go straight on, to go directly to the Lindera pastures and approach the *Salto de la Cabra* ("Goat's Leap") (we imagine that no explanation is necessary as to how vertical these crags are) and rest a while by the winter byres of El Dobrillo, at only 1,050 metres. Well, that's just a manner of speaking, for Beges is just a step away, but at 590 m., and the track leading down there is something of an

adventure poem, zigzagging impatiently down into the valley, with stones, bumps and potholes, but we mustn't panic, the route is very pretty.

The Urdón Canyon, to our left, is promised its own exclusive itinerary, as it holds many adventures in store, together with botanical delights. The beech patches are still with us, as are the hanging fields, the screes and the gorse. The winter byres at Hoja are another necessary stop, allowing us to see the Sierra de Beges from close to, to enjoy the tricks of the light played by the clouds on the crags, to hear the rustling of the leaves blown by the wind and to just sense the wren, sight the black redstart, the rock bunting, linnet and, on any rock, the common wall lizard, while the kestrel seems to hang in the sky.

Arrival at Beges, apart from the satisfaction of having completed the adventure, entails a special visual delight, as it may be the prettiest village of the whole massif, though we certainly do not despise many others dotted around the area. Beges hangs from the mountainside over the impressive Corvera Gorge, with vertical fields behind it, age-old oak and chestnut trees, and a special light at dusk on any day.

After Beges the descent goes on towards the main road, past terraced fields, service trees and the mountain cut vertically, with holm oaks hanging from the side and changing the colour of the rock. Now the path is cement and goes directly to the river gorge, where the white wagtail, the blackbird and the dipper are never far away from each other. The screes are very imposing, the narrowness of the gorge is extreme, and caves and holm oaks are dotted about all around. At the end we sight La Quintana, a village set on green fields and protected by the enormous limestone masses that we leave behind us. The last stretch is the steep slope down to La Hermida, but first we still have to follow the flight of the raven over fields, hazels, chestnuts and service trees so well protected by the crags and beech-clad ridges.

From here it is imperative to go to Panes or Potes to enjoy a well-earned dinner, relive the route over a glass of *orujo** with the jocular comments of our friends and finish off the night with a long and necessary rest.

* See page 239.

Facing page, top: Sierra de Beges • *Middle:* The enchanted village of Beges • *Bottom:* Beges Valley.

THE COASTWARD SLOPES
VI

PANES - MIER - TRESCARES - ARENAS - POO - CARREÑA - ASIEGO - ORTIGUERO -
AVÍN - BENIA - CORAO - SOTO DE CANGAS - COVADONGA - CANGAS DE ONÍS

53 km

This route links the central and eastern massifs from the coastal side of the watershed, and should be done calmly by car or by bicycle, but it is by no means lacking in interest, as we shall go through a charming gorge, which we could think of as a second Cares.

Panes is doubtlessly a great tourist centre, being one of the traditional starting-out points for the conquest of Mt Naranjo. Hotel places have multiplied in recent years and the mild climate of the area attracts visitors over many months of the year. Here we shall make contact with the River Cares, which now carries much more water than it does through Caín, but in a less tempestuous manner. Its waters are no longer green, but they keep their transparency and are well stocked with trout and salmon, as is born out by the fishing-ground signs and the large number of hopefuls who come with their rods in wait for the big surprise, hooking the king of the river, the prized salmon, the impossible dream of so many anglers.

We leave the town by a road with a good surface and limited width

Facing page, top: View from Asiego • *Bottom:* Arenas de Cabrales.

running between the hayfields taking up the valley floor and scattered houses of varying sizes, with an incessant flow of traffic in both directions.

The scenery changes slowly, with the mountains in the background, where the rugged peaks are still crowned with snowy whiteness in the shadows. The trees are scattered, but soon the valley starts to get narrow, the road goes nearer the river and the gallery forest takes on importance, giving rise to a varied fauna.

Holm oaks take over from fields, vertical lines take over from horizontal ones and there is a clear sensation of being in another gorge. The hillsides are covered in heather and the holm oak thickets are denser, the first gullies are to be seen, with screes at their bottoms and the river almost disappears in the shadow of the chestnuts, hazels, willows, service trees and limes. After a bend the first bridge comes into view, by the Molinuca hotel, where there is a car park to leave our car in and start a very instructive walk. A little path goes along the river bank on the other side, where we can observe the vegetation, the devices and ruses of the anglers and the rich birdlife, with the dipper, wren, black redstart, grey wagtail, blackcap, swift, swallow, green woodpecker, blackbird, cuckoo and whinchat. Other animals are also to be seen, such as the Montpellier snake, the common tree frog and the various butterflies that make use of all the flowers along the route. The noise of the traffic does not distract our attention from the path, as the Cares itself takes on the job of filling up the air with its leaps between stones, rapids, widenings and narrowings, where there is an incessant parade of lures for trout and salmon, although the results seem none too good.

The water is transparent but it is beginning to take on the greenish colour typical of the upper reaches, contrasting with a pale-coloured bed that turns dark in the deep pools in the course. In places, the path is about as narrow as a boot, but there is no danger in dry weather if we are careful. Laurels show the dark shades of their leaves and chestnut trees are abundant. Poplars and willows - especially willows - form an actual canopy in some places.

We are soon in Casas de Mier, with its hills covered in holm oak, and a different fauna, worthy of our attention. A bridge over the river allows us to take to the road again (if we take our trip along the path to be over) or to begin a new stretch on foot. Then comes Trescares, with the steep bank of the Rugel on the other side, which waters the tiny Navajo field before giving its waters up to the Cares. This stream is protected by two imposing limestone hulks, Peña Fuentes and Mt Casaspión, which over 4

km form a narrow gorge with holm oaks on the lower parts and beeches higher up, ending at the source of the river, just at the feet of the Tramandón mountains.

The steep slopes meet the salmon river and all kinds of postures are adopted by long sturdy fishing rods to take the attack of the catch. As we advance the gorge gets even narrower, the walls become vertical and the holm oaks grip into any crack. At the riverside, the hazels reach a large size, as do the limes and service trees, while the beeches look over the river course without feeling dizzy. In places the path is lost or goes up and down over rocks where goats climb with a surprising agility, to the envy of some travellers.

The high crags are slashed apart by vertical gullies reaching up to the very summits, with stones falling away to be stopped by the holm oaks covering the lower slopes, while ivy climbs like an experienced mountaineer up the smooth rock faces. The heights are not record-breaking, but

Above: Part of Las Estazadas.

the scenery is worth an outing of its own to enjoy it unhurriedly. At the Oceño crossroads, the gorge starts to widen a little, although the river is still boxed in between the rocks, with bends that make for competition photographs. The rapids are very strong and end up in deep pools in the calmer parts.

We are on the way to Arenas, in more open country, but always accompanied by holm oaks, fields, hazels and the narrow riverside path allowing a different view. Some of the fields seem to be hanging on the cols, and there is a dense gallery forest, well stocked with birds and insects, always against a background of high bastions cut in the limestone. This is the beginning of the Picos, where we can already appreciate the heights of the summits and guess the routes leading up its valleys. Little by little the hayfields get larger, taking up the ever-widening valley, with its high-boled maples, carrion crows and ravens.

Arenas, with its summer bustle, is already well-known to us. Next comes Poo, with its disused copper mines, wide fields and well-kept hou-

This page: The Victory Cross at Cangas de Onís • *Facing page:* Covadonga.
Following double page: Mt Naranjo of Bulnes from the Prayer Well at Poo.

ses. Carreña is a step away, where, in the middle of the village, an unsign-posted road to the right takes us to Asiego. The climb is difficult, with hairpin bends, surrounded by fruit trees and gardens, and with sloping fields. As we gain height, the view of the valley becomes more panoramic, until we reach the village itself. At the entrance to the village, an old man is resting under an apple tree, while an extremely thin old woman, her skin dried up with age, is hardly able to handle the scythe with which she is slowly cutting the grass in the ditch. Houses are numerous, built of stone with wooden balconies, new ones vying with the old for pride of place. Here we have one of the most spectacular natural observation areas of the Picos, commanding views of Mt Naranjo of Bulnes and all its limestone fellows, which on clear days seem to be within the reach of one's hand.

We continue towards Cangas, across a landscape which changes again as we come to fields, mountainsides covered in vegetation, an expanding tourist industry and a good climate. After La Rebollada we cross the watershed, leaving the company of the Cares to follow the Güeña. We are approaching Covadonga, well known to and visited by all hillwalkers, and we go past the Soto detour to carry straight on to Cangas de Onís.

AROUND THE SAJA RESERVE
VII

POTES - FRAMA - CABEZÓN DE LIÉBANA - PIASCA - PESAGUERO - VALDEPRADO -
PIEDRASLUENGAS - SANTA EULALIA - LA LASTRA - SANTOTIS - SARCEDA - COSÍO -
PUENTENANSA - OBESO - QUINTANILLA - LAFUENTE - LINARES - LA HERMIDA -
LEBEÑA - OJEDO - POTES

99 km

Don't be afraid of the distance, this route is designed for those who wish to enjoy a varied scenery without for a moment giving up the comfort of their car, either because the children are too small to walk, because we are feeling the effects of ageing, because of a pregnancy with cravings that need satisfying at once, because of the rheumatism of one's mother-in-law, who nevertheless insists on being one's inseparable companion,

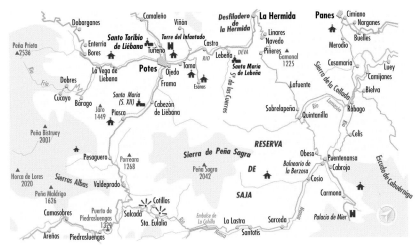

Facing page: Cabezón de Liébana, eternal spring.

187

or simply because we like the technology and air-conditioning of our mechanical emblem.

After a splendid breakfast in Potes, we leave the town in the direction of Santander to go hardly a kilometre down the N-621 past magnificent residences reflecting Cantabrian traditions in building. The first turn-off to the right is signposted to the Piedrasluengas Pass, over asphalt all the way, through fields with little copses, home to the meadow pipit, chaffinch, coal tit, carrion crow, song thrush, buzzard, green woodpecker and great grey shrike, with dense thickets of blackthorn, bramble and juniper, where the field mice hide from the fox, weasel and barn owl. A few clumps of tall pines contrast with the squatter holm oaks. The valley is medium-sized, with green dominating the dark ridges in the background, where beech trees may be made out.

The first village is Frama, its houses contrasting with the pines and holm oaks, taking up part of the valley, great balconies and gardens replete with roses telling us of the area's special climate, and with great stone houses with wooden galleries where the aged vines climb. The fields, large and undulating, are being mown and the smell of hay is in the air. Almost a step away is Vieda, small and spread out over the hillside, with a wood-fired baker's oven ensuring the quality of the bread. Tourism is making its mark on these villages and the offer of apartments for the summer does not go unnoticed. Fruit trees are plentiful, the cherry trees giving a special feel to the wooden walls protecting the fields. Holm oak are still with us in the surrounding area, and the buzzard glides daily over the River Buyón, which is hardly visible because of the vegetation covering it, with willows, limes and ashes boasting their crowns. A few metres further on, a road leads off up to Cambarco, Aniezo and Luriezo, traditional villages from which you can return by an unmetalled road past St Tirso's Chapel to the first junction.

Cabezón de Liébana is a beautiful village with an enormous parish church, old houses still with their wooden galleries and a Roman bridge painted by many artists and covered in ivy, over clear water where we can see a few trout. Decorative and vegetable gardens flourish unhindered as a huge wall of holm oaks keeps the wind off. Peace is absolute, there are few inhabitants and tourism is almost non-existent. We carry on after a look at the Chapel of Our Lady of Carmel.

We must take the turn-off to the right towards Piasca. The road goes

Preceding double page: Piasca *(left).* Luriezo *(top right).* Cabezón de Liébana *(bottom right).*

up to reveal a valley full of fields and scattered houses, with many holm oaks, and buzzards overhead. Mention must be made of the Romanesque church, which also serves as a look-out post from which to see the valley, with heath-covered summits and tributary valleys with elongated fields. The peace experienced invites one to relax.

After Piasca there is a signpost to Los Cos (3.7 km.) and Ubriezo (2.9 km.). After a steep climb we find Los Cos in a large meadow overlooking the valley. It is a small traditional village, untouched by tourism, without even a bar, but with nice people (it only has seven inhabitants) to spend a while talking to. From here we can see Lerones, Barreda and Dos Amantes below in the valley, surrounded by holm oaks and scattered clumps of pines, with well-kept fields and peaks touching the clouds.

We go back down to the road to carry on to Puente Asnil, a small village with an inn surrounded by fields. Soon after we come to Pesaguero, elongated and taking up part of the opposite hillside, in compliance with tradition. We start to climb, the holm oaks next to us all the while, past maples, fields with fences and hedgerows with trees in them, sighting the odd raven, while lizards run across in front of us. We go past Avellanedo on the right, set in a little nook green with fields, the church dominating houses new and old, all of them well kept. The summits are now near, with holm oaks to the left and oak to the right. Cherry trees are still plentiful, as are brambles, and the river is visible down below, with little water and well fringed with river-bank vegetation.

Valdeprado is near the top, with hazels, oaks and tall beeches. The village is small and well kept, with stone houses, and there are abundant elders, bramble and bracken. Nearby, with heather and limestone in the background, we have the Pico Tres Mares (Three Seas Peak, 2,175 m.). A few fields seem simply to appear in the middle of the wood, good places to see a few roe deer, though red deer are not uncommon. The jay comes out in front of us, as do the robin, blackcap, yellowhammer and rock bunting, the ocellated lizard also being common.

Before the top we enter the province of Palencia and there is a turn-off to the left for Puentenansa (34 km.), which we'll take later, as first we're going to the top of Piedrasluengas (1,353 m.) to sit in the wooden observation area and enjoy the fine view (if there is no fog). A track takes us over the rock and fields into a beech wood and along the crest, with views of the Peña Labra mountains on one side and the Cordel mountains on the other. If we follow the road, we'll come to the Palencia village of Piedrasluengas, in the Fuentes Carrionas National Reserve, where we can

admire the valley and the limestone gully in an environment of heather, broom, gorse and hazel.

We retrace our steps to the turn-off to Puentenansa along a none-too-wide asphalt road, its edges colonized by heath, while oaks, holly and asphodel accompany us to the Jabalí ("Wild Boar") observation area, with its view of Peña Sagra (2,024 m.). Following the beechwood, we soon come to the Zorro ("Fox") observation area and then to the Cabezuela Cross, with a view over the valley of Poblaciones, narrow and green, with fields at the bottom. Bends come one relentlessly after another, surrounded by gorse and broom, with blackbirds and jays flying across. To the

Above: The cunning fox.

right at 700 metres is Salceda, almost on the edge of the beechwood, followed by enormous fields bordered by broom and hawthorn. Further on is Santa Eulalia, also on the right, among beech trees and fields where we can see the red roofs of its few houses.

Pesanda has only four big houses and two bars, appearing in the middle of the landscape, with Cablecedo almost next door, where beech, oak, service trees and hazel allow us to enjoy the green fields.

We come to the Cohilla dam, wedged between two limestone masses that seem to be cut vertically, with vegetation growing out of the cracks. The reservoir is small, but the descent to the River Nansa is not at all easy, though certainly spectacular, with hairpin bends taking us into a narrow ravine with beech trees growing wherever they can, gorse, and a dry course. The road narrows and the rocks, previously vertical, are now in horizontal layers, guiding us through the ravine, whose end comes suddenly, with the sight of an open valley. The sides are treeless, doubtlessly to make way for open pastures, now disappearing below bracken and broom, a clear sign of livestock having left them. To the left a track goes off to La Lastra, a little village with a lot of tradition in its old houses. To the right is Tudanca, which has given its name to the breed of cattle grazing in these valleys. The village may be seen from the road, all of it having been declared an ancient monument and enjoying a good state of preservation. The houses aside, the fields around them are in different stages of mowing, creating a beautiful mosaic of shades where green always predominates.

We are soon at Santotis, with the River Nansa below us, a trout stream adorned with riverbank vegetation. Beside us is the gully and all around are clumps of pines and oaks with hillsides transformed into fields. The route continues downwards until we are on a level with Salceda, two hundred metres to the left. This descent into the valley makes the vegetation change, hazels coming to the fore, together with oaks, pines, service trees and bracken.

So we come to Rozadio, on the River Vendel, to continue to Puentenansa, a fine town halfway between the rugged limestone and the Cantabrian Sea, near the Chautín and Micolón caves, and, as is natural in such a situation, it has grown in the shade of an ever-diversifying demand from tourists. On leaving we come to the junction with the road to La Hermida, 30 km. to the right, which we take.

Pedreo is our first contact with a wide valley with fields of long grass waiting to be cut, taking up the sides and tops that our eyes run over.

Then comes Torre de Obeso, a small village comprising a compact group of buildings with one modern house standing out that in no way blends in with the surrounding scenery. We begin the ascent towards the limestone visible in the distance, leaving behind us a once greater wood of oaks and hazel. A goodly number of sheep, all with their black faces looking at the camera, occupy the pastures we go by all the way up to the top. The other side offers us a big valley of fields and villages, all sprinkled with patches of oak, beech, hazel and pine. Sheep walk on the spacious hillsides, and eucalyptus trees are to be seen.

Quintanilla is a large village, combining the traditional, the new and tourism, where you can sense the size of the catering trade, and supply almost meets demand. On leaving we cross the river to begin another climb, still between fields and with the habitual presence of the ravens. Sobrelapeña is obviously a very old village, as is La Fuente, with its

This page: On horseback, the route is seen in a different perspective • *Facing page:* Piedrasluengas Observation Area.

Romanesque (12th-Century) church with a nave without aisles, and surrounded by fields and the rock of the summits. The upward bends follow each other in rapid succession and the hillsides are laden with gorse and bracken that strangle the grass, while remains of the original forest hardly give any colour to the landscape. Streams are frequent, and plots planted with eucalyptus are gaining ground year by year.

Once at the top, the descent before us is steep until we pass Cicera on our left, between the forest and the rock, with high summits, screes and the presence of holm oaks. From this village there is a beautiful walk, suitable only for boots, leading down to the La Hermida ravine. Old mills worth a few photos, an oakwood of enormous trunks and twisted branches, a patch of holm oaks shooting forth from the complicated shapes of the rocks and the possibility of finding redstarts, flycatchers, genets and even an otter are an irresistible temptation for the good naturalist.

Following double page: La Hermida Ravine *(left)*. Sierra de Peña Sagra *(top right)*. Potes *(middle right)*. Liébana Valley *(bottom right)*.

Linares is scattered, almost hanging between fields and ravines, in order to follow the lie of the land round the bends, and we realize that we are quickly returning to the beauty and abrupt slopes of the Picos de Europa. Arriving at Caldas is breathtaking, as the descent is very steep, the bends are very sharp, the road seems very narrow and the vehicles we meet very wide, but me make it without too many problems. At the bottom we can now see the River Deva, flowing through the La Hermida ravine. A boxed-in salmon stream, it waters laurels and buckthorn, willows, ashes and a few alders, while the dipper and the rare otter make their dives. The crag martin, black redstart, ravens and a few vultures may also be sighted.

The ravine is incredible and narrow, with bends displaying the different vertical profiles of the rock, with pools of clean water and fast currents, goats running over the screes, caves housing shadows and the sensation of being in the middle of a huge show put on by nature.

Then the narrowness gives way to the light of open spaces, almost dazzling, with a few cork oaks next to the asphalt. To our left is Lebeña, with the pre-Romanesque church of St Mary, always receiving visitors. Crags and more crags, and the fog begins to blur the silhouettes of the peaks, the rounded fronts of the buildings, the fields and woods, with patches of pine and abundant livestock.

We come again to Ojedo, and from here Potes is a stone's throw, the end of our route, varied in scenery and rich in emotions, and we are sure that we shall relive it more than once fairly soon.

Facing page, top: The valley and the village of Lebeña • *Bottom:* St Mary's, Lebeña.

FOUR ROUTES TO THE BASE OF THE MYTHICAL Mt NARANJO OF BULNES

Five

For many naturalists, hillwalkers, climbers and friends of the impossible, Pico Uriello with its height of 2,519 m. represents the challenge that can never be taken up (only the chosen ones succeed), but at least we can settle for reaching its base, looking at it, saying that up this or that face we would be able to, but at the moment have neither time nor equipment, taking a few photos and returning tired and proud to the car or bus. That's us, but we really enjoy the scenery, which is quite a lot in itself.

The mythical colossus owes its other name of Naranjo ("orange tree") to the fact that the west face, the hardest to climb, on clear days reflects the evening light in unheard-of shades of orange, thus being the flaming emblem of the Picos de Europa.

There are several ways of attacking this limestone hulk from as many different starting points. No adventure is easy, but some of the ways up really are difficult.

Facing page: Mt Naranjo from Pandébano.
Following double page: West face of Mt Naranjo from the Corona del Raso.

FROM SOTRES TO THE URRIELLO MEADOW
I

SOTRES - CABAO BYRES - CANERO WINTER BYRES - PANDÉBANO GAP -
BULNES - BALCOSÍN GULLY - JOU BAJO - CAMBURERO BYRES - JOU LLUENGO -
DELGADO ÚBEDA REFUGE

9 km

We leave Sotres on a clear day, surrounded by green fields and with high peaks ahead. We follow the road down to the last bend, by the Cabao winter byres, to cross a swollen and torrential River Duje by the Moyeyeres stone bridge. The clear waters let us see a bottom of rocks of varied colours, almost a premonition of the changes in scenery awaiting us. We start the climb, on a broad path that winds its way up the hillside as it widens our view of the Sotres Valley and the Duje Gorge. The slope is not very steep, and we can keep up a good rhythm. We soon reach the bottom of Cueto Cuaceya (1,088 m), with a view of the whole of Sotres and of the valley side that ends at Caballar Col.

Keeping close to the Canero brook, we come to the winter byres of the

Facing page: Mt Naranjo from Pandébano, north face.

205

same name, with Pandébano Gap (1,224 m.) a step away. Behind us, on the opposite side, is Sotres, and nearer to us are the rolling fields with their scattered winter byres, in perfect condition, with cows and horses not very far away from goats and sheep. Next to the sheds, the cracks in the crag support grass, heath and juniper. The black redstart, kestrel and buzzard are easy to spot. From the col, Mt Naranjo can now be seen in the background, with its unmistakable profile of vertical lines, with limestone masses and snow patches all around, but nevertheless, the centre of attention of all wayfarers.

From the col to Bulnes (La Villa) the route is gently downhill all the way, past the summit of Maín (1,595 m.) on the left, where a few vultures take advantage of the thermals to glide around and soar effortlessly. We shall soon leave the stony ground for the grass around the winter byres of Jabariega, with those of Cantiello nearby, the mountainsides covered with grazing land and livestock and, naturally enough, the odd horsefly, which starts a few arms waving about when it comes near.

We get to Bulnes, that is to a quarter called La Villa ("The Town"), which is only a few metres from the other quarter, El Castillo ("The Castle"), to which it is linked by the Colines Bridge and a similar way of life. The ensemble is charming and compact, its houses keeping the traditions that time has waylaid for ever, the whole watched over by the rustic chapel where the prayers of climbers are almost a must before they go out to meet the colossus.

In the village bar, we have a cool beer and enjoy a natter with the locals, whose stories about the harrowing moments most of them have lived through in the rescue of mountaineers in difficulties will make you realize just how hard the climb is, and how necessary it is to be careful in the utmost, as changes in the weather can be as sudden as they are unforeseen. Don't lose heart, however, for the actual ascent to the foot of Mt Urriello is about to begin.

We leave Bulnes (La Villa) to follow the track by the river, reaching the Mestas waterfall and the Voluga de Canti-Sierra, where one's legs feel heavy and breath is often short, to start up the no-less-steep Balcosín Gully, to carry on past the Jou Bajo and reach the Camburero winter byres, in a corrie surrounded by high rocks that block our way in all directions, except one, straight to our objective. Having got our strength back, we continue up and round the mountainside to the Peña de las Cuestas ("Crag of the Slopes"), certainly an appropriate name given the climb ahead, where the contour lines seem to run into each other. After a slight gentleness in the climb, we come to other steep stretches (we're 1,700 m.

up), which only level out slightly near the end, close to the Delgado Úbeda Refuge. Our first stop is at the fountain, where we drink carefully as the water is cold from the melted snow and from the clear nights. Then time stands still for us to admire the scenery. We are now in the heart of the Picos, where nature has conferred the sensation of wildness on every chiselling of the rock faces. Every gully is full of screes, vegetation is scant and the air is both cold and almost non-existent, and the silence is broken only by the cry of the choughs. We are now at the feet of Mt Naranjo, which we can actually touch. Yet it is not just a huge pyramid-shaped limestone mass with obvious difficulties for the climber, especially on the west face, which has a sheer drop of 600 metres, or indeed the north face with the E*spolón* ("Spur") jutting out from it in an overhang. Neither is it just the story of its conquest on the 5th August 1904 by Pedro Pidal, the Marquis of Villaviciosa, and Gregorio Pérez, the "Cainejo*", or the prowess of Alfonso Martínez ("Big Fonsu"), who reached its summit more than a hundred times, or the unwritten names of all those who have been up it or rescued those who have failed in the attempt. It is, above all, letting our feelings flow freely in its contemplation while we pay it our respects.

* *Cainejo* = an inhabitant of Caín.

Above: Bulnes, where, to the urban mentality, life seems impossible.

TO THE URRIELLO MEADOW FROM PONCEBOS
II

ARENAS DE CABRALES - PONCEBOS BRIDGE - LA JAYA BRIDGE - JARDU BRIDGE - EL TEJO BROOK - COLINES BRIDGE - BULNES - ACEBUCO BYRES - TÍES COL - CAMBURERO BYRES - URRIELLO MEADOW

14 km

Our proposal for this route is to set out from Arenas de Cabrales, which is already familiar from other adventures, a tourist centre replete with rucksacks, boots and staves every day in summer. We can drive from here to the La Jaya bridge, which saves us having to walk 7 km. over easy country between fields with the River Cares beside us, and with the ever-present never-ending limestone as a backdrop for everything. We go through a small gully into which the River Praón spills its waters, go past

Above: The way up to Bulnes. • *Facing page:* View of Mt Naranjo from Camburero.

The map contains the following labels:

a Sotres — CUETO VIERRO 1165 — CABEZA DE LA MESA 1605 — MAJADA DE LA TENEROSA — Refugio de la Tenerosa — SIERRA DE LA CUADRA — PEÑA DE MAÍN — Cuesta Sierra — Collado Vallejo — INVERNALES DE ARNANDES — PEÑA CASTIL 2444 — Jou de los Machos — TORRE NAVARRO 2602 — PEÑA VIEJA 2613 — MONTE TOLOBRE — RÍO DUJE — COLINES 1463 — Canal de Balcosín — Jou Bajo — Jou LLuengo — NARANJO 2519 — LOS CAMPANARIOS — TORRE DE LOS HORCADOS ROJOS 2506 — a Arenas de Cabrales — Puente del Jardu — LA VILLA BULNES — Canal de Camburero — MAJADA DE CAMBURERO — VEGA DE URRIELLO — PUENTE PONCEBOS — Riega del Tejo — Puente la Jaya — Murrallón de Amuesa — Canal de Amuesa — El Bohío — CUETOS DEL ALBO 2445 — Refugio Delgado Úbeda — Jou Sin Tierre — Jou de los Boches — NEVERÓN DE URRIELLO 2559 — TORRE DE LA PARDIDA 2596 — TIRO DEL OSO 2576 — PICO TESORERO 2570 — La Raxuca — CARES — Jou LLuengo — Hoyo de Cerrero

the Obar winter byres on the left, past the power station outside Camarmeña and to the confluence of the Cares and Duje.

To the left of the bridge a path leads off to the river, where we soon find another bridge, Jardu bridge, which takes us across to climb up a steep slope which is short but very hard on the legs. Then we follow the El Tejo brook, a gentler climb by the water where we are distracted by lizards and beetles and by the sparrows, wagtails, redstarts, kestrels and ravens flying around us. We then cross the Bulnes river by the Colines bridge to reach the Barrio del Castillo ("Castle Quarter") of Bulnes and admire its stone houses with their wooden galleries, photogenic nooks with clogs outside the doors, hazel switches shiny from the rubbing of the stockman's hands, the sound of bells round animals' necks, firewood piled up to stoke the stove on cold days and the warm welcome of the locals, accustomed to the sight of hundreds of wayfarers walking between their houses without stopping anywhere.

The second place is La Villa ("The Town"), where the path starts almost between the houses to take us to Mt Naranjo, the climb (about 4.5 km) beginning in the actual village. We leave the green areas behind for the rock, where the path is stony up to the Acebuco byres, now more than 1,300 metres up. Then comes the Tíes Col and a steep but short rise to the Camburero byres. We have gone the whole way parallel to the previous route, that is with the Balcosín Gully on our left. From the byre the walk follows the route already described, any further explanation being obviously unnecessary.

Facing page: Poncebos *(top)*. La Jaya Bridge *(bottom)*.
Following double page: Mt Naranjo from the Camarmeña Observation Area.

TO THE URRIELLO MEADOW FROM THE CABLE OBSERVATION AREA
III

CABLE OBSERVATION AREA - HORCADINA DE COVARROBIES - PEÑA VIEJA - HOYO SIN TIERRA ("CORRIE WITHOUT EARTH")- CABAÑA VERÓNICA - JOU LOS BOCHES - LOS BOCHES GORGE - JOU SIN TIERRE - URRIELLO MEADOW

5 KM

It is perhaps one of the least known routes, lacking the tradition of the previous ones, but the gentleness of the ascent (in comparison with others) and the continuous descent from Horcados Rojos to the Urriello Meadow make it the obvious choice for those who wish to reach Mt Naranjo with their bodies less shattered by the hike.

We take the cable car up to the Cable observation area, the same as when we go up by 4WD. On arrival, a group of nuns hurry out of the cable car, obviously impatient to soak up the spectacular views of the Picos. The accent of their laughter sounds familiar, South American. Overflowing with joy, they start a battle (a friendly one, of course) with snowballs flying in all directions, freezing their hands and waterlogging their feet.

Facing page: Cable Observation Area.
Following double page: Mt Naranjo from Horcados Rojos.

We move away from the holy hubbub to start the walk that will take us to the feet of the venerated Mt Urriello.

From the observation area, the path hugs the rock till it gets to the Horcadina de Covarrobies, where it forks. The left-hand fork leads up to the peaks, stopping at La Vueltona. We are right by the Old Crag (2,613 m.), impressively high and its summit almost hidden by clouds. From here on, wheels replace boots and horsepower replaces the will to get there. We go past the Jou sin Tierre to begin an ascent that isn't too steep

to begin with, but then zigzags up to the base of the Horcados Rojos, a limestone monolith standing imperturbable before us. Choughs are abundant, vultures are sometimes to be seen in the sky and there are chamois resting in sunny areas of sparse grass or walking over the screes to lie down under the protection of the crags. In summer, there is a stream of visitors going along the path in both directions, vying with each other

Above: Madejuno from the Jou sin Tierre.

in speed, design and colour of their mountainwear, in their Japanese cameras and, above all, in the colourful vocabulary used to express the admiration aroused in each of them by the scenery. It is just a step from here to a continuous descent to the Cabaña Verónica Refuge, and all around us the endless limestone hulks struggle for prominence in shapes, height, hues, slopes, snow patches, *tornos**, gullies and an endless list of further details that make it necessary to visit the area every year.

We are now going down, gently at first, to reach the feet of Los Urrieles (2,551 m.) and Pico Tesorero ("Treasurer Peak", 2,570 m.), then a bit steeper down to the Jou de los Boches and an effortless stroll past such major mountains as Mt Tito Navarro (2,601 m.), Mt Tiro de Santiago (2,440 m.) and Los Campanarios (2,670 m.) and come to the Los Boches Ravine. Here, there is a more panoramic view, with the dip of the Jou Sin Tierre, towards which we direct our steps. To the right is Las Moñetas (2,554 m.) with the Urriello Meadow below and Mt Naranjo ahead of us. The refuge is a step away, and this is without a doubt one of the easiest routes.

* See note on p. 161.

___

This page: The Cabaña Verónica Refuge • *Facing page:* The Forgotten Crag from La Vueltona *(top)* and Horcados Rojos *(bottom)*.

TO THE URRIELLO MEADOW FROM CAÍN
IV

LA JARDA WINTER BYRES - CASIELLES BRIDGE -
DOBRESENGROS GULLY - HOYO GRANDE ("THE GREAT CORRIE") -
ARENIZAS COL - JOU SIN TIERRE - URRIELLO MEADOW

10 km

This route will only be touched on at the most interesting points, as it is one of the really hard ones, so it is only for the specialist and for those desperate people who feel the need of a proper adventure, where they can put to the test not only their physical condition, but also their sense of direction, as over many of its stretches the track is absolutely invisible. If you are decided to bring off this feat, get yourself a good set of maps, compass and rucksack, and all the necessary for any unforeseen event and, above all, try to persuade other adventurers to suffer with you.

The route begins at the winter byres of La Jarda, a little before Caín de Abajo, or at the Casiellas bridge, after the village. In either case we shall

Facing page: The ever-challenging Mt Naranjo of Bulnes, or Mt Urriello.

come to the Casiellas stream, which we shall follow up as far as La Espi-
pera, where we cross it to enter the Dobresengros Gully, a hard trip, which
only the old hands manage to do in one go. For lesser mortals, stops are
frequent, which lets us enjoy the view of the valley, take in how far up
we've come and, what is worse, reckon how much we have left. At 1,900
m. the slope levels out a little and we have a bit of let-up as we go past
Hoyo Grande Bajero ("The Lower Great Corrie"), reach Hoyo Grande
Cimero ("The Upper Great Corrie"), and go over the Arenizas Col to the
corrie of the same name, where we have Mt Naranjo in front of us. The
climb has been quite stunning, but now we have quite a descent to the
Jou Sin Tierre, which is almost next to the shelter. The route is certainly
worth the effort if you are hooked on mountains, peaks, difficult walks,
chest-bursting climbs, loneliness, and the sensation of having found a
different world in which to pit your strength against Nature's, or if you
have any other excuse, but you should always remember that quite a few
mountaineers have gone missing round here. In any event, depending on
your own circumstances and whims, you can always count on the help
and advice of professionals, either in León or in Potes, Arenas or other
parts of the Picos de Europa.

NOTES FOR TRAVELLERS

Six

This purpose of this last chapter, or at least the author's intention for it, is to sum up the information given throughout the book, add a little more that had no specific place and provide a ready reference for all those readers who like soaking up the nature of the Picos de Europa.

Equipment, Clothing and Behaviour

Such an apparently silly thing can help bring off a memorable day of enjoyment or clash totally with the paths and observation areas offering us all the beauty of the mountains.

Changes in the weather can be sudden in Picos, so, we shall take the liberty of recommending one or two things designed to ensure the success of our outings.

Hillwalkers should always wear comfortable and loose clothing and put waterproof capes in their rucksacks just in case. Flexible thick-soled footwear is basic if we are going to avoid the irritating little stones besieging our feet. Sunglasses and sun tan lotion should be inseparable trekking companions, as should a hazel stick, with or without a ferrule, but straight and dry. The ideal length is up to the chest (your own, that is).

You should always take the maps appropriate to each route, available at any reputable bookshop. With the aid of a compass and an altimeter, you will be able to get out of complicated situations, such as fog or nightfall, when they overtake you earlier than expected.

No nature lovers should leave behind their field guides to the flora and fauna, as much enjoyment is to be gained identifying the many different species, some of them unique to these mountains. Binoculars make good company (8x30 or 10x30 will suffice), and for the unconditional photo buff, a close-up lens for detail and a telephoto lens (400-600 mm) for chamois, roe deer and, with a lot of luck, perhaps even a bear.

We realize that the rucksack is a very personal thing, something like our own privacy that we take with us, brim-full of useless knick-knacks as heavy as stones that we'll never use, but each traveller is a world unto himself, to be respected.

Facing page, top: Going up to Horcados Rojos • *Bottom:* In the Jou de los Cabrones.

Respect scrupulous and devotional is of the utmost necessity for those who wish to be considered adventurers, travellers or tourists. By this we mean the best manners towards the path itself (4WD fans beware - don't ignore any signs and don't get the bit too firmly between your teeth), towards plants that must not be pulled up, towards animals that must not be disturbed and towards winter byres and huts that deserve the same respect as palaces. Well, we suppose the message has got through.

The Orography of Picos

The mountainous massif of the Picos de Europa constitutes a clearly defined geographical unit between the sea and the Cantabrian Mountains, divided between the provinces of Asturias (districts of Amieva, Cangas de Onís, Cabrales, Peñamellera Alta and Peñamellera Baja), Cantabria (Tresviso, Peñarrubia, Cillórigo-Castro and Carmaleño) and León (Oseja de Sajambre and Valdeón).

The estimated area is 574.86 square kilometres and heights above sea level vary from the 2,648 metres of Torre Cerredo to just 90 metres in the lower reaches of the River Cares.

The network of rivers divides the area into three massifs:

▨ The *Eastern* or *Ándara* Massif, bounded by the Rivers Duje, Nevandi and Deva, whose highest points are Tabla de Morra Lechugales (2,441 m.) and Pico Cortés (2,370 m.)

▨ The *Central* or *Urrieles* Massif, between the Duje and the Cares, which includes the highest points in the region - Torre Llambrión (2,642 m.), Torre Cerredo (2,648 m.), Peña Vieja ("The Old Crag", 2,613 m.), Pico Tesorero ("Treasurer's Peak", 2,570 m.) and the most emblematic summit, Mt Naranjo of Bulnes (2,519 m.).

▨ The *Western* or *Cornión* Massif, between the Cares and the Dobra, whose highest points are the impressive Holy Crags (Peñas Santas) of Castile (2,569 m.) and Enol (2,478 m.).

Two great canyons border the rock colossi: the Sella to the west, in the Los Beyos Gorge, and the Deva to the east, in the La Hermida Gorge. The characteristic nakedness of the area's peaks contrasts with the luxuriance of the surrounding valleys. Snow may be seen on the summits all the year round.

At heights of over 2,000 m. there are no springs or running water. Water from melted snow seeps down through the permeable limestone to the lower, impervious layers, bursting forth in powerful springs which give rise to spectacular waterfalls, but not before wearing away the innards of the crags and forming grottoes and caves yet to be explored.

Yet the two characteristic features of Picos scenery are the gorges, or ravines, and the corries (*jous*), which confer a lunar appearance on the landscape.

Ravines are the paths opened up bravely by rivers in deep cuts, boxed in by enormous rock walls where verticalness vies with awe-inspiring overhangs, and where the vegetation is varied, abundant and characteristic of the area.

Corries are enclosed depressions, which are dry and practically free of vegetation, formed by quaternary glacial action aided by underground streams.

Owing to the limestone nature of the area, there are no large lakes, except Enol and La Ercina in the Covadonga area, and the Pozo de Ándara in the Eastern Massif.

There are no glaciers, only permanent snowfields of varying sizes - pride of place going to the 1.5 km length of the Transllambrión in the Central Massif and the 1-km-long one on the north of the Holy Crag of Castile. The rest are small, and dotted around the sides of corries and mountainsides sheltered from the sun.

The area has a varied and extensive network of rivers which seems designed to flow through each part, in harmony with the surroundings, with gentle courses in low-lying areas and wild and crazy torrents roaring down from the crags in unrepeatable waterfalls, streams and tributaries, with innumerable lesser courses, some of which are still apparently unnamed.

Picos is full of wide meadows and pastureland, with both long and short grass, intense green or dry, dotted with shepherds' and cowherds' huts always ready to receive the wayfarer during storms, with native woods of beech and oak, where the lime, chestnut, gorse, holly, maple, ash, birch, hazel, plum, holm oak, cork oak, laurel and strawberry tree add colour, volume and feeling to an unrepeatable environment, changing with the seasons, yet timeless.

Wildlife is abundant and varied, different on the crags and in the valleys, characteristic in the gallery forests, special in every nook. The chamois is practically the standard on the crags, while the roe deer prefers the woodland shade and the meadows of the valleys and the red deer is lord of the heather. The griffon vulture shows its silhouette daily, while the golden eagle is meaner with its appearances, as is the peregrine falcon. The wolf, now legendary, still roams the tracks and wanders through the tales recounted in front of the fire. But surely the two greatest stars of Picos are the capercaillie, with its aura of a gallant lover that every spring attempts its conquest in the heart of the wood, and the bear, part myth, part reality, a coming together of ferocity and tenderness, once persecuted without truce, now revered and in danger of extinction.

The list of species would be almost endless, with pine martens, beech martens, otters, polecats, foxes, weasels, genets, wild cats and wild boar among the mammals, and goshawks, kites, kestrels, snipes, barn owls, little owls, long-eared owls, Egyptian vultures, ravens, choughs, jays, black woodpeckers, kingfishers, snowfinches, wallcreepers, dippers and many others representing birdlife. To enter into the world of insects is to lose oneself among myriad species with eye-catching colours, shapes, sizes and behaviour. The discovery of the life of each route is the priceless reward offered to us by Nature in the Picos de Europa.

Lakes and Ponds

Set right in the middle of the Picos de Europa National Park are two fine lakes: Enol and La Ercina, both over 1,000 metres up.

Lake Enol shows its glacial origin and reflects the mountains in its 12-hectare surface, with pure and cold waters that become dark at the maximum depth of 23 metres. *Lake La Ercina*, also glacial, is smaller (8 hectares) and much shallower (3 metres), its clear waters forming a nook where rest is what first comes to mind. Both are reached from the Covadonga Shrine by a made-up road where the slopes and bends monopolize the driver's attention for 12 kilometres.

Lake Bricial, 1,130 metres up, occupies a small glacial hollow at the base of the ascent to the peak of the same name. Near to the two already mentioned but considerably less well known, it is worth the wayfarer's trouble to stop and look.

Carmen Pond (Laguna del Carmen), near the King's Observation Area, also inside the Park, is about 1,200 metres up. Although it is small, it is very beautiful, and surrounded by a rugged landscape where one stretches out one's resting time without having to be asked, while trying to fix every nook indelibly on the retina.

In the Central Massif there are very few lakes, at least large ones, but one we will find there is *Lake Las Moñetas*, at a height of 1,700 metres, near *Mt Escamellao* (2,010 m.) in a landscape of naked rocks and crags, where the chamois are reflected in the sparse water used to refill many walkers' bottles.

Llagu Raso is 1,860 metres up and comes after the Camburero Gully if you set out up Mt Naranjo of Bulnes from Bulnes village. It is surely a good place to meditate on the difficulty of some of the routes, when the legs are already tired from the effort and the throat cries out for a good drop of cool water.

Lake Amuesa is right by the winter byre and protected to the north by the great wall of Amuesa. We can get to it if we leave La Villa (Bulnes) and head for the Amuesa refuge via the gully of the same name, on one of the classical Picos routes.

The four *Lloroza Ponds* are 1,800 metres up in the limestone with chamois as their backdrop and the sky within reach. They may be reached from the Cable observation area heading for the Vueltona. In summer, when they may be dry, their beds become a camp site for a goodly number of visitors.

Llago Cimero and *Llago Bajero* (the "Upper and Lower Lakes") give water to the Asotín Brook, at the feet of the Colladinas and on the route to the Collado Jermoso shelter. The grazing land on its banks invite one to camp there, sharing the land with the livestock.

In the eastern massif, two names are familiar: one is the *Pozo de Ándara*, next to the Mazarrasa mines and near the Casetón de Ándara refuge, on the route from Sotres to Beges. The volume of water in it has decreased immensely owing to mining work, but the spot is still one of the most beautiful of the lesser known nooks of the massif.

The other is the *Llago de Valdominguero*, whose name is longer than the body of water itself, though it is an ideal place for rest in the solitude of the mountains.

Smaller ponds with local names frequently appear on each route, some of them dry, others no more than puddles, most of them tiny dewponds, each with its own appeal, all receptive to our rest or siesta. Asking about their names is a good way to start pleasurable conversations with shepherds and locals.

Rivers

▓ The *Sella* rises at Fuensella, sheltered by the valley of the Pontón Pass, to collect the frozen water of the famed Hell Spring (Fuente del Infierno). This thread of water receives nourishment between the environs of Pica Ten and beyond the village of Vierdes from streams of Barreyo Gap, Valdelafuente, Neoncito, La Capitana, El Joyo, Potingos and Hueso. At the Venta de Cobarcil it is joined by the River San Pedro, where it begins to get boxed in, to flow oppressed down the Los Beyos Canyon. At Puente Angoyo, in Asturias, it is joined by the Rivers Ponga and Dobra, its flow-rate increasing and its tempestuousness diminishing. It is joined by the Güeña at Cangas de Onís and reaches the sea at Ribadesella, where it forms a wide and peaceful ria, home to a goodly number of bass, sea trout and gulls. This is after 65 kilometres of constant change, the banks it waters ever more luxuriant.

It is a historical river, witness to the struggles between Cantabrians and Asturians, legendary for its salmon and famous for the traditional canoe race taking place amid much pomp and merry-making on the first Sunday in August from Arriondas to Ribadesella, which arose from a bet between friends at Infiesto some years back.

▓ The *Dobra* hardly babbles around the Vegabaño and Carombo byres to enter the Angón Valley, dominated by the panoramic view from the Ordiales observation area. It is briefly detained by the Jocica dam to receive a little further on the Toneyo, bringing the waters of the Batuta Spring. To the left it gives up its waters to the River Pelabarda, which takes the liquid element and the popular legends of the Great Spring (*Fuentona*) of Fana, to subsequently increase its volume with the waters of the Rivers La Beyera, Pomperi and Junjumia. It may not be so famous as the Sella, but the spots it waters have a delicate beauty worthy of many and lengthy visits.

▓ The *Cares*. Divides the Urrieles and Cornión Massifs. This mythical river rises in the upper part of the Valdeón Valley to cross thick beech woods where the noise of its waters consoles the lonely wayfarer. From the Pandetrave Pass it receives the waters of the Serena Brook, which joins it at Posada de Valdeón. After Cordiñanes it enters a short spectacular gorge, a foretaste of the veritable banquet of crags and drops in store in the Cares Ravine, or "Divine Gorge", a marvel worked by nature's eternal chisel over long years.

The River Bulnes hands over the water of the Urrieles to it at the La Jaya Bridge, those of the Duje joining it at Poncebos Bridge, its descent calmed as it flows through small gorges before reaching the village of Arenas de Cabrales. Here it is joined by the Casaño, forming salmon pools of great beauty, to empty out at Puente Lles, after 54 kilometres of adventures.

▓ The *Duje*. Rises at the passes of Áliva from the Resalao Spring on the Old Crag (Peña Vieja), collecting in its first stretch the cool and fresh waters of the Vidrio Gully. It divides the Central and Eastern Massifs, flows calmly past the Sotres meadows, where it disappears in summer, to reappear by the Tejo winter byres. After the village of Sotres, it becomes faster on its way down to Tielve, where it forms a backwater amid luxuriant vegetation. Its short length of 18 km contrasts with a vertical difference of 1,500 before its confluence with the Cares at the Poncebos bridge.

▓ *Deva*. From its source in the Fuente Dé corrie it goes down the Valdebaró Valley, where it collects the waters of Liébana. The Nevandi comes down to it from the Áliva Passes and it takes on the waters of the Ándara Massif. At Potes and Ojedo it is joined by the Quiviesa and the Buyón. The Rivers Coruera and Urdón join it at La Hermida, forming a long narrow ravine with a Mediterranean climate, to reach the valley of Panes, where it is joined by the Cares on its way north to the sea.

Gorges and Ravines

▓ *Divine Gorge of the Cares*. A classic and compulsory walk in the Picos de Europa, it is formed by the River Cares between the villages of Caín, in León, and Puente Poncebos, in Asturias. It starts at Posada de Valdeón, to form a little later the Foz de Caín, the anteroom of the gorge itself, both of them deep and narrow cuts in the limestone to separate the central and eastern massifs. On reaching the district of Cabrales it forms the less well known Foz de Rumiá and Canal Negra, which are less spectacular but which afford nooks protected from the curious where the vegetation and wildlife decorate the landscape with wonderful colours.

▓ *Foz de Trescares* is at the village of the same name in the district of Peñamellera Alta, where the Cares shines as a salmon stream with pools, boxed-in rapids and wider stretches between thick gallery forests.

▓ *The Duje Gorge*, near Tielve and Poncebos, in the Cabrales district, is between the great rock buttresses of Peña Maín and Portuera, in Puertos de Era.

▓ *The Indias Gorge* is formed by the Duje, as are the *Allende* and *Aquendi* gorges, is near to those already mentioned and, therefore, to Tielve and Sotres, in the Central Massif. They are small secluded gorges, each with a different appearance identifying it as a representative of a definite scenery type.

▓ The *Estazadas Ravine* is between Ortiguero and Carreña, where the River Casaño opens up the crags to flow unseen from the road.

▓ The *La Hermida Ravine*, another famous name, is on the edge of the Eastern Massif linking the towns of Potes and Panes, and so used by the road. The River Deva flows through it. The length of this gorge, the sheer sides, the overhanging vegetation together with the cascades and backwaters of the river make it a must to see.

The *Urdón Gorge* is on the Tresviso, between the Cocón, Macondiú and Beges mountains in the Eastern Massif. It is somewhat off the beaten track, so it is only visited on purpose. It is deep, not very long but very abrupt and poor in vegetation and wildlife but creates a different view amid a scenery of mountains, rugged peaks and green valleys.

Foz del Nansa, near Beges and La Hermida. It is a cult to the lovers of pure limestones, with imposing screes that seem to want to block the river, emptying out into wide meadows of long grass.

Los Beyos Gorge, where the Sella plays hide-and-seek with the bends and crags, hiding from the wayfarer or showing off the ferocity of its waters. It joins Asturias with León and is the route from Riaño to Cangas de Onís.

Santa Bustia Ravine, formed by the river of the same name from the village of Viego and Puente Vidoso, near Los Beyos. It is in the Ponga district, at the feet of Peña Salón.

Los Andamios Ravine, formed by the River Cándano around the foothills of Peña Salón between the villages of Viboli and Cándano. Its position below the western massif, in Asturias makes it look incredibly wild in such tame surroundings.

Tejo Gully, formed by the River Bulnes between Poncebos and the village of Bulnes itself. It is the natural division between the Great Wall of Amuesa and Peña Maín (Central Massif) and ends by joining the Cares Gorge.

Observation Areas (Miradores)

Every higher area of land, every gap, pass or peak is a natural observation area with unforgettable views. Some of these places, however, are famous for truly spectacular panoramas. We now mention a few of those that all travellers agree about regarding the wonder of the views they offer:

Asturias

Ordiales Observation Area, in the National Park, after the Vegarredonda refuge. The emplacement of the inscription to the memory of Pedro Pidal commands the Valley of Angón and the whole spectacle of Picos. There is a 1,000-metre sheer drop, which is surely a sign of its privileged situation.

King's Observation Area (Mirador del Rey), overlooking the Pome beechwood. Easy access by a track from Lake Enol.

Queen's Observation Area (Mirador de la Reina), right on the road from Covadonga to the lakes. Beautiful views of the Sierra de Cuera and even the Cantabrian coast.

Prince's Observation Area (Mirador del Príncipe), recently built to permit detailed views of the Comella Valley and where information panels tell us about the process of disappearance of the glacial lakes.

Camarmeña, traditional view of Mt Naranjo. Reached from Puente Poncebos after a walk of barely a kilometre

Prayer Well Observation Area (Mirador del Pozo de la Oración), at Poo de Cabrales. It is a monument of homage to Pedro Pidal and the "Cainejo", with unbeatable views of Mt Naranjo, with the Casaño in the foreground

León

Vista Alegre, right on the road from Oseja to Soto de Sajambre, by the entrance to Picarancón tunnel. Its panorama of the San Pedro Falls are justly famous, as is it views of the valley.

❀ *Santa Marina*, at Pandetrave Pass. Unsignposted, but with wide views of the Friero and Bermeja.

❀ *Piedrashitas*, also known as the "Wind Flute" because of the metal sculpture dominating it. From the widened area at Panderruedas a path leads off which brings us after ten minutes' walk to this observation area. Fine views of the Western and Central Massifs and a wide panorama of the Valdeón Valley.

❀ *Valdeón*, A short distance down from Panderruedas Pass going towards Posada de Valdeón. Commands a view of the whole valley, where beechwoods cover mountainsides and summits and a sizeable clump of holly trees varies the colour of the landscape.

❀ *El Tombo*, or the Chamois observation area, where the statue of a chamois has been photographed by thousands of visitors on their way to the Cares Gorge. An information panel gives the names of the main peaks.

❀ *Llesba Col*, dominated by a whitish statue of a bear, symbol of the Cantabrian Mountains. From the top of the San Glorio Pass, a 2-km track leads off to its base. Commanding views of the Fuente Dé Corrie, the Cereceda Valley and the district of Liébana. Surely one of the finest natural observation areas, where the views can only be taken in if we scan carefully from one side to the other.

Cantabria

❀ *Santo Toribio de Liébana*. Panoramic views from the wayside chapel of St Michael at St Toribio's Monastery. From here the Fuente Dé Corrie seems to be within arm's reach, and the valleys may be identified from their meadows and woods.

❀ *El Cable*, or *La Lloroza* at the upper station of the Fuente Dé Cableway. A balcony of transparent ironwork projects over the abyss to impress the traveller with a spectacular panorama of the Valdebaro valley, Peña Remoña, Horcados Rojos and myriad other summits. Only chamois and choughs, apart from visitors, reach such heights.

❀ *Pilate's Balcony Observation Area (Mirador del Balcón de Pilatos)*, by Tresviso, at the feet of a breath-taking cliff. View of the Deva Gorge.

❀ *Pandébano*, near Sotres, reached by a wide track, well used and in good condition. Surely one of the most visited, as Mt Naranjo here is an almost palpable reality, as it shows its west face to the camera lenses.

Towns and Villages

The tiniest hamlet, far from any route or lost among the mountains, offers the traveller hospitality with the special character of the mountain folk which is an unmistakable part of the human geography of Spain. For this reason we shall only mention the larger places, those offering more to the tourist in general, and those that are communication centres on any of our routes.

Asturias

❀ *Cangas de Onís*. The seat of the Onís district, it is the most important town in the Asturian mountains, and is the departure point for Covadonga. In summer it receives a huge number of tourists, who find good catering and a lively atmosphere in its streets.

It was made a city by King Alfonso XIII and was once the seat of a monarchy in the reigns of Pelayo and Favila. It is surrounded by the rivers Sella and Güeña, and its emblem is the Roman bridge, from which the Victory Cross hangs.

❀ *Arenas de Cabrales*, at the confluence of the Rivers Casaño and Cares. It is the departure point for the conquest of Mt Naranjo or the Cares Gorge, and the undisputed capital of the Cabrales cheese area. In summer, it attracts many tourists, who find all they need in its shops and are able to enjoy a privileged climate.

▓ *Panes*, the capital of the Peñamellera Baja, where it straddles the River Deva. It receives a good number of tourists, in search of either mountains or beaches. Catering is good, as is the local gastronomy, a temptation for the most demanding stomach.

León

▓ *Riaño*, or the New Riaño, a village of modernist design overlooking the waters of the reservoir. Its vocation as a tourist centre is born out by the services it offers. Its position on the approach to the mountains attracts many people in summer.

▓ *Oseja de Sajambre*. Capital of the Leonese mountains and almost at the beginning of the Los Beyos Canyon. Its mild climate keeps the landscape green nearly all year and it is a departure point for many outings. Traditional food combines with accommodation for different types of tourism.

▓ *Posada de Valdeón*. The permanent guardian to the Cares Gorge and a meeting point for thousands of tourists and centre for camps, excursions and walks around the Picos. Its privileged position is not matched by the number of hotel rooms, although the friendliness of the locals sometimes makes up for this shortcoming. It has a Red Cross post. Mention must be made of its *hórreos* (see p. 234).

Cantabria

▓ *Potes*. The real backbone of mountain tourism, for which it is ideally suited because of the climate resulting from its low height and its position right in the middle of the Picos. The traditional, well-kept architecture, its colonnades and the whole historic and artistic ensemble make a visit to the town a must. Those who enjoy typical mountain food will find all they need to satisfy them here, together with sufficient good accommodation. It is the capital of Liébana and as such is an active commercial, political and social centre.

▓ *Cosgaya*. Though small in size, it is big on catering. It is on the Deva, surrounded by little valleys eating back into leafy beechwoods, and has well cared-for livestock and solidly built mountain houses.

▓ *Espinama*. Between the Deva and the Nevandi Rivers, a rural centre given over entirely to tourism. From here it is possible to reach the Áliva Passes and conquer Mt Naranjo.

Mountain Refuges

There are not very many, at least not considering the large numbers of visitors now coming to the area, but they are situated at points that are exceptional as far as scenery is concerned. It is recommend to find out in advance if it possible to stay the night in one. Some, the minority, have no warden or bar, and are left open and are at the mercy of the crassness and lack of education of those who seek to pass as hillwalkers. It should never be forgotten that apart from offering shelter and rest to adventure lovers, they can also save lives when the weather catches us unawares with one of its sudden changes. We must all insist on civilized behaviour.

THE WESTERN MASSIF

▓ *Vegabaño* (León). At 1,340 m. in the shadow of Mt Cotorra, at the Vegabaño byres. It sleeps 27 and has a warden and a bar. Guides may be engaged for walks and climbs. It is the property of the León Mountaineering Federation. Unsupervised camping is permitted nearby.

※ *Vega Huerta* (León). At 2,010 m. at the foot of the Holy Crag of Castile. The property of ICONA (see p. 239), its state of neglect make its ten berths only relatively useful.

 ※ *Vegarredonda* (Asturias). At 1,550 m., near the Llampa and Cimera Peaks. Its large capacity (70 places) makes it one of the most used by groups. It has a guard and a bar and is the property of the Asturias Mountaineering Federation.

 ※ *Ordiales* (Asturias). The property of ICONA, with 6 cement bunks, fireplace, table and broom.

 ※ *Municipal Shepherds' Home* (Asturias), at 1,080 m. in the Enol Meadow. Property of the Cangas de Onís Local Council. Sleeps 20, well kept.

 ※ *Vega de Ario* (Asturias), at 1,610 m., next to the Jultayu Peak, the property of the Asturias Mountaineering Federation. Fifty places, warden and bar.

 ※ *Frade* (León), at 1,700 m. at the base of Peña Bermeja. It is the property of ICONA, sleeps six and is in a very bad state.

CENTRAL MASSIF

 ※ *Collado Jermoso* (León), at 2,064 m. at the feet of the Llambrión. Sleeps 20, warden and bar in summer.

 ※ *José Ramón Lueje* (Asturias), at 2,080 m. in the Jou de los Cabrones and near Torre Cerredo. Property of the Asturian Mountaineering Federation. 14 places and a warden in summer.

 ※ *Delgado Úbeda* (Asturias), by the mythical Mt Naranjo, at 2,050 m. Property of the Asturian Mountaineering Federation, with 90 places, warden, bar and a degree of luxury (hot water).

 ※ *Terenosa* (Asturias), at 1,315 m., at Pandébano, overlooking Bulnes village. Property of the Asturian Mountaineering Federation. 30 places. warden.

 ※ *Áliva* (Cantabria), refuge and *Parador* (state-owned hotel), at 1,670 m., with 50 places, restaurant and hot water in summer. Property of Cantur.

 ※ *El Cable* (Cantabria), at 1,845 m., sleeps 16 in bunks. On the ground floor of the bar of the cableway station.

 ※ *Cabaña Verónica* (Cantabria), refuge/camp at 2,325 m at the foot of the Tesorero. Sleeps 6, warden in summer. Property of the Cantabrian Mountaineering Federation.

 ※ *Vigón* (Asturias), hut/camp at 1,425 m. at the base of the Great Wall of Amuesa. Property of the Asturian Mountaineering Federation, with 15 places and a warden in summer.

EASTERN MASSIF

 ※ *Casetón de Ándara* (Cantabria), at 1,730 m., next to the Sacred Heart on the Ándara meadows. The scenery is wonderful, but the refuge is open, neglected and in bad condition.

Places of Historical or Artistic Interest

Many and varied are the places we could mention, but the list would be very long and would not fall within the scope of this chapter, which would lose its usefulness. It would be advisable to consult specialist literature, although we shall call attention here to certain details, beginning with rural architecture, typical mountain houses, stone walls, wooden balconies and roofs of fired tiles. Each province has its own style, as the traveller will notice.

Especially noticeable are the *hórreos*. In León province they are considered the insignia of the valley, about fifty original ones being preserved, mainly at Posada, Santa Marina and Soto. They are now considered historical and artistic monuments and, as such, enjoy the corresponding official protection. The main material used in their construction is oak, as it withstands the weather for many years. The base may be square, with four legs, or rectangular, with six. The legs (called *horcones* or *pegollos*) are pyramid-shaped oak logs standing on thick stones (*plintos* or *machos*). They are topped off with large flat stones (*tornarratas*) that are wider than the legs themselves, to keep the mice out. The floor is made of oak planks, as are the walls, where they are arranged horizontally, the ends sticking out at the corners. The door is small and the structure is used as a grain store. The roof is usually tiled and has four inclined faces. Stone steps, which do not enter into contact with the structure of the *hórreo*, lead up to the door. A limited number of *hórreos* (in Caín and Oseja) have an exterior corridor.

Hórreos were built with the enforced help of all the local people, the owner having to feed them meanwhile. The amount and type of the meals were laid down by law, and wine never ran short.

Asturian *hórreos* are built in the same way, except that the wall planks are placed vertically, and the roof may be covered with slate, or thatched with rye grass, perhaps even with broom.

Asturias

▓ At *Cangas de Onís*, there are several things to see: the *Roman bridge* (so called although it is in fact Gothic) of the 14th Century, with three arches and a height of 20 metres in the centre, where the Victory Cross hangs. The 18th-Century Baroque style *Soto Cortés Palace*, at Labra, retains the wooden gallery and the heraldic shields, and is home to the Ethnographic and Archaeological Museum. *St Eulalia's Church*, at Abamia, still preserves part of its pre-Romanesque Asturian structure. Worthy of note is the side door, with strainer arches. The *Ermita de la Santa Cruz* (Chapel of the Holy Cross), at Contrequil, 2 km from Cangas, is a national monument, built over a dolmen which can still be seen inside. It is dated AD 437. However, in 737, King Favila had it altered to commemorate the Battle of Covadonga. Also here is the *Cueva* (Cave) *de los Azules*, a prehistoric burial site (closed to the public).

▓ *Monastery of St Peter at Villanueva*. (2 km. from Cangas) A Romanesque national monument, built in 746 at the behest of Alfonso I. It is in a secluded spot, where great lime trees offer a fine shade for meditation. The east end, with three apses and barrel vaults, still survives. The rest disappeared after the rebuilding of 1687, the south doorway being particularly noteworthy, with hunting scenes thought to represent King Favila's famous struggle with the bear.

▓ *Buxu Cave*. Near Cangas, it contains cave paintings showing a variety of animals including red deer, bison, goats and horses.

▓ *The Royal Site* (see p. 239) *of Covadonga* and *Holy Cave*, better known as the Cave of the *Santina*. Under the slopes of Mt Auseve, there is a natural cave with a great waterfall, where the Virgin appeared before King Pelayo, who began the unstoppable Reconquest. The *Santina* is a polychromed wooden carving of the 18th Century dressed in silk and gold, and set on the stone altar. A clear indication of Asturian devoutness is the fact that the 103 steep steps up to the cave are often climbed by pilgrims on their knees as a penance or a promise, hence the name Stairway of Promise. At its foot is the Fountain of Marriage, tradition having it that if you drink from each of its seven spouts, within a year you will meet a marriage partner. The water runs into a pond where visitors throw coins as a promise to return soon.

▓ *Collegiate Church of St Ferdinand*. Mention must be made of its cloister of square columns and the door with grilles through which the old burial vault may be seen. The old part houses the Inn.

▓ *Basilica*. Begun in 1887 and inaugurated in 1901. It takes up an enormous flat space on the side of Mt Cueto, and has fantastic views. The groundplan is a Latin cross, with a nave and two aisles, with three apses. The two high towers are clearly visible, the whole ensemble being built of pinkish marble. It houses the figure of Our Lady, by Sansó, and the Cross of Victory, by Miranda.

▧ *The Church of St Mary of Llas*, Arenas de Cabrales, with a nave without aisles in three sections, barrel vault and columns with attractive framed capitals sculpted with animals and plants. The original structure dates from 1385.

León

▧ *The Wayside Chapel (Ermita) of Our Lady of the Pontón*, at the Pontón Pass. A solidly built stone construction with a rectangular groundplan and a graceful belfry, with a barrel vault at the east end.

▧ *Assumption Temple*, Oseja. A huge solid Romanesque-Byzantine building with a Latin cross groundplan, with the tower finished off with a semicircular dome visible from most parts of the valley. Archbishop Caneja (an illustrious local surname) had it rebuilt with stone from the nearby Vierdes quarry, whence the contrasting brown and grey hues. Next to it is the Great Walnut Tree (*Nogalón*), an impressive tree of great age giving shade to the games of skittles.

▧ *Crown Chapel (Ermita de Corona)*, Cordiñanes: 18th-Century, small, with two storeys and a tower with an *espadaña* (see p. 239). It takes its name from the coronation of King Pelayo after the Battle of Covadonga. It is isolated among the meadows and surrounded by woods and crags, in charming scenery.

▧ *Chorco de los Lobos* : A peculiar and unique construction for catching wolves, it comprises a circular trap made of stones (the "well") situated at the bottom of the valley at the end of a V-shaped stockade leading up to the crests of the valley. When a wolf was sighted, the bells were rung to call everyone to the compulsory hunt, which consisted in luring the wolf into the stockade, reinforced with brambles to keep it in. Also inside, in a few little huts made of thick branches, a number of locals would lie in wait to goad the wolf into the well with sticks. Once inside the stone trap, it was finished off by some of those taking part, its skin later exhibited in neighbouring villages, where a collection was taken. An information poster leaves one in no doubt about the system. (At present it is in a state of disrepair).

Cantabria.

▧ *Santo Toribio De Liébana* (3 km from Potes), 8th Century, founded in the time of Alfonso I, although some expert opinions consider its origins to go back several centuries further. A detailed visit will show us several architectural jewels, like the church, a Gothic building erected on the site of a Romanesque one and since altered several times. Worthy of note are the Door of Pardon (16th Century), the Chapel of the *Lignum Crucis*, or of Christ's Cross (18th Century), containing the most important relic of the wooden cross. The chronicles say that this wood was sawn into two parts in the 16th Century to make the present cross. The last alteration, carried out in the 1950s, changed the medieval appearance of the church. There is a nave and two aisles with ribbed vaults and three polygonal chapels. The Door of Pardon is Romanesque and is only opened during Holy Years. The main doorway has a round arch and archivolts. *St Catherine's Chapel*, 12th Century, is in ruins, but its position at the top of the hill makes it one of the best places to observe the valley and the Fuente Dé Corrie. *The Holy Cave* is a pre-Romanesque chapel partly hewn from the rock of Mt. Viorna, a nice walk from the monastery.

▧ In *Potes* we can visit *The Infantado Tower*, a 14th-Century fortress of the Marquises of Santillana del Mar, in the middle of the town. Today it houses the town council and the Crafts School (*Escuela Taller*), which produces excellent guides for the Cantabrian Mountains. The 15th-Century *Orejón Tower* has a beautiful doorway emblazoned with the heraldry of the nobility, and a solid well-preserved wooden door. *St Vincent's Church*, with a Romanesque base but late Gothic (14th Century) structure, has a nave without aisles and a side chapel.

※ *St Mary's Of Lebeña*, in Lebeña, is a 10th-Century Mozarab church, with a rectangular groundplan, a nave in six sections, barrel vaults, and horseshoe and round arches. From the outside it looks like a building divided into a large number of rooms, in a magnificent state of preservation and an incomparable natural setting. Beside it is a gorse bush as old as the church and an olive tree that is no younger. The 18th-Century image of St Mary is a polychromed carving with a special charm.

※ *Casona*, Tama, an imposing stately building vying with the medieval bridge as a subject for many painters.

※ *Military Academy*, Colio. The front and the entrance are preserved, in beautifully placed stone, with a shield. It was in use during the Peninsular War. The village is well worth a visit as it retains the traditional style, commands a panoramic view over the Liébana valley and is surrounded by large oakwoods.

※ *Parish Church*, Ojedo. 12th-Century doorway, and in a part of Cantabria unmarked by the passage of time. See also the singular Narezona Chestnut Tree, with a perimeter of 13 metres at the very stingiest estimate, and an age difficult to reckon.

※ *St Mary's Church*, Piasca. A beautifully preserved Romanesque church whose façade is certainly worth a few photographs. Today it has a barrel-vaulted nave (without aisles) with lobulated arches. The lovers of sculpture have the opportunity of admiring several pieces - on the South, or Horn Doorway, the hunt of the wild boar is depicted, while the west face has 13th-Century sculptures of St Peter and St Paul and a 14th-Century one of the Blessed Virgin - while nature lovers may enjoy unrepeatable views of the valley.

※ *Medieval Tower*, Mogrovejo. Well preserved and covered in ivy. The whole village is very typical of the area and the emblazoned houses make beautiful photographs.

※ *Tudanca*. This village has been declared an ancient monument in its entirety. It is set in the valley amid well-mown terraced fields.

Some Festivities and Romerías (see p. 239)

If there is one thing that the folklore of this region is known for, it is the feasts and popular *romerías*, with both religious and pagan elements, combining church services with gastronomy, dances and cattle markets, cheese and craft shows, folk customs and tradition dress, indeed, quite an attraction for the visitor wishing to understand the character, behaviour and customs of people who still live in harmony with the rugged, generous, harsh and unrepeatable environment of the Picos de Europa.

We must by no means scorn family festivities, like the slaughtering of the pig, the hay harvest or the local saints' days, when the doors of every house open to invite the visitor in to share in the life of the locals, all for nothing in return except a respect for their traditions, which are, at the end of the day, just as valuable a source of information as nature itself.

※ *January*

St Sebastian's Day in Ojedo, on the 20th. A popular festival.

St Vincent the Martyr's Day, on the 22nd, at Cillórigo and Potes, where it is surely the most popular festival in the town.

※ *February*

St Eulalia's Day, on the 12th, at Abamia. Popular festival hardly involving any outsiders, a true reflection of the character of the area.

※ *May*

Livestock fair at Potes on the 1st, with a show where the best animals, farm equipment tools and typical regional produce are on sale.

The feast of the *Santuca*, at Potes on the 2nd, where religious festivities are prolonged with pagan activities.

🌑 *June*

St Anthony's Day, the 13th, at Covadonga, and on the 29th, *San Pedro de Villanueva*, with a great show the day before, with the traditional floating bonfire on the River Sella.

St Peter's Day, the 29th, at Potes, with religious celebrations, and a busy market for the farm produce and craft products of the valley.

🌑 *July*

The day of Our Lady of Health, or the *Santuca* of Áliva, on the 2nd on the pastures of Áliva, where a pilgrimage to the wayside chapel precedes the popular *romería*. There is an important rally of horses and riders and the scene is dominated by the character of the herdsmen.

St Marina's Day, the first Sunday, celebrated simultaneously at Posada de Valdeón, Prada and Los Llanos, the number of visitors at each place changing each year according to the attractions. At Santa Marina de Valdeón, the feast is celebrated on the 18th, when the local people congregate around the church.

The Lakes, on the 25th, also called the Herdsmen's Feast, with a great *romería*, where the shepherds and herdsmen decide on the use of the grazing lands. There is a traditional race up to the *Porra* (knoll) of Enol.

🌑 *August*

The Snows, on the 5th, at Soto de Valdeón. A feast of great popular tradition, where visitors are warmly welcomed.

Celtic Night, at Corao at the beginning of the month, with all the historical influence and local additions that you can imagine.

Descent of the Sella, or the Festival of Canoes, on the first Sunday. It starts at Arriondas and finishes at Ribadesella. It is surely the international Asturian festival *par excellence*, where hundreds of thousands of visitors follow the paddlers' journey down the river. We recommend the train journey, which allows for stops where you can enjoy good cider and admire the scenery (and do whatever else you need to do). There is an epic feast at the end, which lacks absolutely nothing.

Our Lady of Valmayor, on the 15th, at Potes, with the feast of Our Lady on the same day at Beges and Turieno. These fiestas link up with the following day without a break.

St Roch's Day, this saint being immensely popular among mountain folk, is celebrated on the 15th at Oseja de Sajambre, Panes, Tama and Pido among other places. Good humour, cold meats and wine are present in all of them. At Arenas de Cabrales, the *corri-corri* is celebrated, experts believing it to be of prehistoric origin and linked to a phallic rite. The *bailín* (a male figure dressed in red) is surrounded by six young women carrying laurel branches who dance in a circle and pretend to run away for him to follow them.

Cheese fair, on the last Sunday at Arenas de Cabrales. It is an extremely popular festival, with displays by folk groups and the election of the *Pastora Mayor* (the oldest shepherdess or herdswoman still working) and of the *Xana* (see p. 239) *del Naranjo* (the most attractive of the young women present, always a difficult decision).

St Tirso's Day, on the last Sunday at Ojedo, with a well-established and well-supported popular *romería*. There is a picnic, which is not to be missed.

🌑 *September*

Our Lady of the Way, on the 8th, in Potes, a perfect combination of the religious and the mundane.

Our Lady of Corona, on the 8th, at Posada de Valdeón, Caín and Cordiñanes, where religious fervour leads to a *romería* of great tradition.

The *Santina*, on the 8th, at Covadonga, when Asturians and others come to pay homage to their most loved Virgin.

Santa Cruz (Holy Cross) on the 14th, at Potes, where the festivities last for several days, which gives rise to many possibilities, including a picnic.

Our Lady of Health, on the 24th, at Caño, with participation by the locals in an almost unique atmosphere.

▓ *October*

Cheese fair, on the 12th at Cangas, where craftwork is the centre of attraction, as is the mixture of mountain dialects, which will delight the visitor.

▓ *November*

All Saints' Day, the 2nd, at Potes (and in a great many villages), where the village folk rally in a markedly religious atmosphere.

▓ *December*

The Immaculate Conception is celebrated in every village, in each in its own way, so the mentioning of individual places would only disorientate the reader. May each one choose those factors that he finds most interesting, and he won't be disappointed.

A note about Cheese and *Orujo* (see p. 239)

To speak of food and drink in this section would imply writing a whole new book, and one that would barely scratch the surface. Who hasn't enjoyed the *cocido* of León, the *fabada* of Asturias or the *caldereta* of Liébana? (see p. 239) To speak of meat and fish would be to talk of quality and the love going into the preparations of the dishes, the contrast of mild and strong flavours, the subtlety and blatentness of a cuisine occupying one of the top positions in world gastronomy. We shall only mention, then, just in case someone out there hasn't found out yet, a tiny part of that culinary wealth, cheeses and *orujos*, which have brought - and are bringing - fame to the Picos de Europa region, and which are enjoying a good reputation beyond its borders.

▓ *Los Beyos Cheese*. It is made in nearly all the villages next to the gorge, Viego being one of the biggest producers, although it is also made in the Sajambre Valley. It used to be made with goat's milk, but now cow's milk is used. Goat's milk cheese can only be obtained at Canisquero, in Ponga and Pregondón, in Amieva. The cow's milk ones may be distinguished by their yellow colour, those made of goat's milk being much paler. In some places it is made with ewe's milk. It used to be the custom to smoke this cheese, though today this is not always done. They are small cheeses with an irregular cylindrical shape, due to their home-made nature. The smell is not strong, but gentle on the palate, though the cheese is rather dry and compact. Ideal for dessert with preserves or jam.

▓ *Picón Cheese from Valdeón*: It is made from a very mature *Cabrales*-like cheese mixed with very hot boiled milk and *orujo*, the mixture being kneaded to form a soft paste which is kept in an earthenware pot. After a month and a half it takes on a greeny-bluish veined appearance, the result of fermentation. It has a very strong flavour and is ideal spread on a few good slices of *hogaza* (see p. 239) bread. It is wrapped in maple leaves. A home-made variation consists in putting the remains of cheese as it is eaten into an earthenware pot containing *orujo*. After a few months, the resulting mass has an extraordinarily strong flavour.

※ *Posada de Valdeón Cheese*: Made from cow's milk, though it may also be made from goat's or ewe's milk, it sets in tin moulds which are later covered with plane or maple leaves and left in a cave (or a cellar) for six months. It is a cheese for spreading, with a strong flavour and sharp smell.

※ *Cabrales cheese, from Arenas de Cabrales*: Its production gives work to a great many families in the region, each one varying the proportions of cow's, goat's and ewe's milk. Peculiarities of its making are the use of *cuayu* (natural rennet from a cow that has just calved), a few pieces of a lamb fœtus, and fermentation in high-altitude caves facing north. It isn't an alchemist's recipe, but a genuine and renowned cheese. The caves, with temperatures of about 4°C and constant humidity, are usually shared by several families. The cheeses are stacked and take at least three months to ferment properly. Annual production is about 60,000 kg for the whole district. A few years ago, the cheeses used to be wrapped in cabbage leaves, aluminium foil now being used.

※ *Pido cheese*, made from cow's, ewe's and goat's milk. Semi-cured, soft and slightly sour. Whole cheeses are small.

※ *Smoked Liébana cheese*, made from cow's, goat's or ewe's milk. Medium size (1.5 kg.) and strong flavour. Smoked with juniper wood.

※ *Quesucos*, small flat cheeses, made from cow's, ewe's and goat's milk in different proportions. Made in Lebeña and Espinama.

※ *Beges cheese*, included under the controlled appellation of Cantabria cheeses, home-made from cow's milk. Medium flavour and somewhat pasty.

※ *Peñamellera cheese*, a cottage cheese made from cow's milk. Small, with a very mild flavour.

※ *Liébana orujos*. Under this name there are varieties for all tastes: *El Coterón* from Santo Toribio is especially famous as a pure *orujo*; honey *orujo* has a mild flavour but is not exempt of degrees; *herb and bilberry orujos*, the latter to be found in many private houses, with a strong, somewhat bitter flavour and a blackish-mauve colour. There are also home-made *orujos* of all kinds with spectacular flavours, such as blackberry, onion, lizard, fig, chestnut, walnut, in short a whole range of innovations with greater or lesser success, which sooner or later will have to be tried.

*Translator's note*s:

ICONA: See note on p. 75.

Espadaña = Typical Spanish belfry consisting of one wall with gaps to house the bells, which are visible from both sides.

Romería = a short local pilgrimage.

Xana = the wood nymph of Asturian and Leonese folklore.

Orujo = a spirit made from distilling the grape skins left over from wine-making.

Cocido = a stew comprising mainly chickpeas and different meats, *fabada* = a stew based on white beans and different types of pork products, and *caldereta* = (roughly) casserole.

An *hogaza* is a roundish loaf with a fairly hard crust and an interior which takes longer to go stale than that of a stick-type loaf.

*the printing of this book was
finished on st isidro's day,
15th may, 1996*